SHREWED

A WRY AND CLOSELY OBSERVED LOOK AT THE LIVES OF WOMEN AND GIRLS

• ESSAYS •

ELIZABETH RENZETTI

ANANSI

Published in Canada and the USA in 2018 by House of Anansi Press Inc.
www.houseofanansi.com

House of Anansi Press is committed to protecting our natural environment. As part of our efforts, the interior of this book is printed on paper that contains 100% post-consumer recycled fibres, is acid-free, and is processed chlorine-free.

22 21 20 19 18   1 2 3 4 5

Library and Archives Canada Cataloguing in Publication

Renzetti, Elizabeth, author
Shrewed : a wry and closely observed look at the lives of women and girls / Elizabeth Renzetti.

Issued in print and electronic formats.
ISBN 978-1-4870-0304-3 (softcover).—ISBN 978-1-4870-0305-0 (EPUB).—ISBN 978-1-4870-0306-7 (Kindle)

1. Women—Social conditions. 2. Women's rights. 3. Feminism.
I. Title.

HQ1155.R45 2018   305.4   C2017-904729-9
                    C2017-904730-2

Library of Congress Control Number: 2017947362

Book design: Alysia Shewchuk

We acknowledge for their financial support of our publishing program the Canada Council for the Arts, the Ontario Arts Council, and the Government of Canada through the Canada Book Fund.

Printed and bound in Canada

For my mother, the light at one end of the tunnel,
and my children, the light at the other

CONTENTS

INTRODUCTION:
TALES FOR YOUNG WITCHES

MY PATH TO liberation began with one profane word written on a fat pink eraser. I was probably alone, as I often was in those days, sitting in the school library, where all young heretics learn their first and best lessons.

How old would I have been? Perhaps nine or ten, grade three or four. I loved the library; it was a sanctuary and a theme park, a cocoon and a spaceship. I was sitting on the carpeted steps, staring at the bookshelves the way a drunk stares at the rows of bottles in a liquor store. Which one would I read next? Perhaps it was time for a mystery featuring Alfred Hitchcock's Three Investigators. Or a new Beverly Cleary. I'd already read every one of Walter Farley's Black Stallion books.

Idly, I sat on the steps with one of the library's erasers in my hand. I have always been a doodler, and I began to write on its soft pink surface, so lovely and yielding. It needed to be clearly marked as library property, or someone might steal it. I scanned the library shelves as my pen moved, and after a few minutes I looked down at what I'd written on the eraser. My breath stopped in shock.

In thick blue letters I'd written LIB.

I clapped my hand over the eraser and looked around the library in panic, frightened that someone had seen the terrible word. Fortunately, I was alone. It was the mid-seventies: the librarian—a young woman with long hair and a plaid miniskirt—had probably stepped out for a smoke. Smoking and ignoring children were two of the great pastimes lost with that decade.

I looked down at the eraser. I'd meant to include the whole word "library," but the eraser was too small. And "LIB" was awful. I'd heard adults talk about *women's lib* with scorn and contempt in their voices. My father dismissed any females he disliked, flatly, as "women's libbers." I wasn't sure what "lib" meant, but it must be very terrible indeed. Quickly, I drew a box over the word and began filling it in, ferociously scribbling till you couldn't see the word at all. There. I'd erased it. I'd erased us.

How did I get from there to here? From being terrified of a word because it was associated with female emancipation to becoming a feminist newspaper columnist? I grew up in a family that had very little money, in which the words "women's lib" were profane. My father was in many ways an unorthodox thinker, yet he carried his family's Old World values like an identification card: He taught his sons to play chess, but not his daughters. He gave us different curfews. He made my sister and I get rid of our one-piece Speedos, which were as provocative as burlap sacks, because he felt they were too revealing.

And yet—and yet. My sister became a lawyer. I became a journalist. I worked my way into the middle class, and words that were once blasphemous became my gospel. Along the way, I've been harassed and groped and shushed, but I've also been encouraged and mentored and promoted.

I have no creed in this world—no religion, no ideology—except feminism. It is an essential part of my being.

As a journalist, I have spent nearly thirty years reporting on other women's stories and listening to their challenges, failures, triumphs. I've written about how the world fails women, systemically, even now, when the playing field is supposed to be level. I've interviewed astronauts and midwives, scientists and soldiers, survivors, politicians, painters, novelists—each one a hero of her own story. These women forged paths, gained wisdom, learned which bridges harboured trolls, which berries were safe to eat and which would send them into a hundred-year sleep.

Centuries after our struggle for emancipation began, women's ambitions continue to inspire fear. Our requests to share power are rebuffed. Yet we consolidate wisdom, we find strength in sisterhood, and for this progress we are viewed, like the witches of old, with a mixture of fascination and dread. To the chagrin of the witch-baiters, we persist. Every young witch explores a different road. I'm going to follow some of them in this book. First, I'll start with mine.

In university I earned a nickname. One day in politics class, our professor—a South African exiled for his political beliefs, on whom I nurtured an intellectual crush—broached the topic of abortion rights. At the time, the Supreme Court of Canada had not yet struck down the country's restrictive abortion laws, and reproductive-rights campaigns were active and vocal.

The classroom stirred to life. We were all studying journalism and liked to hear our own voices. One of my classmates waved his hand frantically, desperate to speak his piece on women's reproductive freedom. Let's call him "Tool" for the sake of brevity.

"There wouldn't need to be abortion at all," Tool said, "if women would just carry the babies and give them away to couples who want them. Think of all the people who can't have babies of their own. Everybody wins."

I seethed with rage. My hand shot up. "That's ridiculous," I spat. "Women aren't *walking incubators*."

My classmates giggled. Thereafter, I became known as "Inky," shortened from "incubator." As a journalist's nickname, it wasn't too bad. I carried it as a badge of honour.

But, like many young women, I was a mass of contradictions. During the day, I was Inky, the take-no-prisoners advocate for women's rights. I was the Women's Issues reporter for the university newspaper, writing about discrimination on campus and Take Back the Night marches. At night, though, when the pub closed, I went home with vampires. I spoke up loudly in class but fretted, quietly, that this would make me unlikeable.

More than anything, I struggled with the inherent contradictions of journalism. Despite our reputation for cynicism, most of us become journalists because we want to change the world in some way, as trite as that may seem. We're like tiny models of the Earth: one centimetre of cynical crust on the outside, tons of gooey sentiment on the inside.

Yet we're meant to control our innate idealism. Worse, we're meant to hide it. Objectivity and neutrality were the gods we bowed to when I was in journalism school, and although the understanding of journalists' relation to the material world has changed in the decades since, there is still a prevailing sense that journalism and advocacy are uncomfortable bedmates. We're supposed to choose one or the other, and a journalist who is also an advocate is considered a tainted version of both.

It's taken me decades to resolve these contradictions in my own head. Years ago, my friend Kim and I attended a pro-choice rally for the National Abortion Rights Action League. We both worked for different newspapers as junior writers, and we spent the day running away from news cameras and hiding behind trees, terrified that we'd be spotted and reported to our superiors. There are codes of conduct, some written and some unwritten, that prohibit journalists from advocacy.

But I soon realized that I could be an advocate for the cause I believed in. I could do it by my presence, as a female columnist in a male-dominated industry. I could do it in my choice of subject matter, highlighting the system-deep oppression of women in Canada and beyond. And, if I were funny, if I could make people laugh, maybe readers would listen.

"DO YOU KNOW ANY FEMINISTS?" My son asked me this question one night over dinner. At the time he was thirteen, and genuinely curious. I looked over at my husband, who was trying not to laugh (he is a stellar man, but he knows how this will set me off and he does love fireworks).

I set my knife and fork down, and managed not to scream. My daughter, four years younger than her brother, looked at me curiously. I tried not to think about the entirety of my mothering years being a dismal failure. Instead, I said, in a strangled voice, "Yes, I do. Me, for example. I'm a feminist. And Dad. And your aunts and uncles, and your grandmothers, and all my friends, and...everyone. Pretty much everyone we know."

"No, not like you," my son said, shaking his head. "Like *real* feminists."

What did he mean by this? What was a real feminist to him? As a young teenager, he existed, perilously, between the actual world—where his mother told him that interrupting his sister is a gendered act—and the online world, which was possibly more real and certainly more entertaining. The online realm was a subterranean goblin-zone where feminists were considered witches and bitches and worse. My boy was wise and tolerant, even at that age; yet even he was confused.

I stared at my children over the dinner table wondering, not for the first time, where I'd gone wrong. Did I not buy them enough neutrally coloured clothing when they were infants? Did I not point out the sexism in every ad we ever saw on TV? Did I not say "she" when we talked about scientists? Did I not buy my daughter enough construction toys, my son enough dolls?

I was clearly a bad feminist. It was a crushing realization. At the time I was reading Roxane Gay's wonderful collection of essays *Bad Feminist*. It offered some balm to my soul, which strives for ideological purity but still has a ring around its collar.

Gay writes: "I am a Bad Feminist because I never want to be placed on a Feminist Pedestal. People who are placed on pedestals are expected to pose, perfectly. Then they get knocked off when they fuck it up. I regularly fuck it up. Consider me already knocked off."

Gay tumbled off her pedestal because she is "a woman who loves pink and likes to get freaky and sometimes dances her ass off to music she knows, she knows, is terrible for women and who sometimes plays dumb with repairmen because it's just easier to let them feel macho than it is to stand on the moral high ground."

I'm a bad feminist because I enjoy *The Bachelorette* and read historical romances. I do not know how to change a tire and feel my time on earth is too short to learn. I wear high heels, even though I realize they are bad for my feet and good for the patriarchy.

In the past seven decades, thousands of books and academic articles and newspaper stories have been written on the subject of what was once called "women's liberation" — those terrifying words — and now is called "feminism." At the beginning of the first volume of *The Second Sex*, Simone de Beauvoir writes: "I hesitated a long time before writing a book on woman. The subject is irritating, especially for women; and it is not new. Enough ink has flowed over the quarrel about feminism; it is now almost over: let's not talk about it anymore. Yet it is still being talked about. And the volumes of idiocies churned out over this past century do not seem to have clarified the problem." That was in 1949. Almost seventy years ago! Simone might be astonished to witness the debate that still rages.

We've had more waves than an ocean. We've had more voices than a Coke commercial teaching the world to sing. We've heard that feminism has been co-opted by capitalism, that it needs to be more inclusive, that it has failed to adequately address issues of racism within its ranks, that it has an identity problem, that it's no longer necessary. I think all of those are true, except for the last.

I like to think of contemporary feminism as a garden. On the surface, where the flowers bloom, all seems healthy and vibrant. I mean, look at all the empowerment campaigns by yogurt companies telling us to love ourselves! Look at the fashion designers who send out young, rail-thin beauties wearing shirts that say "feminist" onto the catwalk! Look at the adorable babies in their "This Is What a Feminist Looks Like" onesies!

"All of these things reflect feminism's inroads into mass culture, but it's still unclear what happens to feminism once it's there," Andi Zeisler writes in her 2016 book *We Were Feminists Once: From Riot Grrrl to Covergirl®, the Buying & Selling of a Political Movement.* "Marketplace feminism is seductive. But marketplace feminism itself is not equality."

Zeisler draws a distinction between empowerment on an individual level, which feels awesome and fuels a great number of advertising campaigns, and the much more intractable issues of power, dominance, and representation. On a more systemic level, women are still undervalued, underpaid, and underrepresented in public life. We still suffer unacceptably high levels of sexual violence and partner violence. We are harassed in offices, on the streets, and online. Our voices and clothing choices are judged and found wanting.

And it is women who have been traditionally left out of the feminist movement — women from racialized communities, trans women, women with disabilities — who suffer most from these power imbalances. Over the years, they've been twice rejected: by the hierarchies that oppressed them in the first place, and then by feminist allies who excluded them. At the beginning of the twenty-first century, feminists have begun to realize that they need to amplify different voices in order to survive.

Over the years that I've been writing about women's issues, many things have gradually improved. But in the period I wrote this book, gathering new information and reading news stories and reports every day, I was staggered at how little progress we've made in some areas. There were many days that I rolled around in a slough of despond, with little but *The Bachelorette* to improve my mood.

On the subject of equal pay — an ideological minefield, by the way — my colleague at the *Globe and Mail*, Tavia Grant, reported this in early 2017: "Recent annual data show that, in yearly earnings, women working full time in Canada still earned 74.2 cents for every dollar that full-time male workers made. Another measure that controls for the fact that men typically work more hours than women—the hourly wage rate—shows women earned 87.9 cents on the dollar as of last year."

In the United States, the former Secretary of Labor Robert Reich talks about how the wealth gap—how much women own compared with men—is even more serious than the income gap. He estimates that women in the U.S. own 32 cents of wealth for every dollar a man does. For women of colour, the gap is worse.

There is the issue of the word itself. In a poll of a thousand forty-something women conducted in 2015 by the Canadian magazine *Chatelaine*, fully 68 percent of respondents did not consider themselves to be feminist. (Interestingly, a poll in the *Washington Post* in the same year found that 60 percent of American women considered themselves either "feminist" or "strongly feminist.")

I'll admit that this denial of the very essence of feminism enrages me. I know it shouldn't, because I believe in freedom of expression, but my God, ladies. Were they not looking at the same information that I was? Every day, I read about high-profile sexual predators being set free by juries of their peers. Women and girls murdered by their partners, even after they'd repeatedly warned the authorities that they were in danger. Female politicians subject to misogynistic taunts. The toxicity of tech culture is evident in the harassment and discrimination lawsuits that litter Silicon Valley. As I wrote this book, a deluge of stories broke, all centred on serial sexual harassment perpetrated by powerful men. Even moments of progress were coloured with sadness: A long-overdue inquiry into the horrendous abuse faced by Canada's Indigenous women and girls—more than 1,200 of whom have been murdered or gone missing in the past four decades—got off to a troubled start in 2016, an unsettling development for the women's families.

And, of course, at the end of that year, the world's wealthiest and most powerful country elected a poisonous misogynist over one of the best-qualified candidates to ever run for president. That seemed to prove once and for all that Depeche Mode were right when they sang "God's got a sick sense of humour."

I don't believe in God, though, so I don't even have that for comfort. I used to believe in the essential rationality of the human project, but my faith in even that has been shaken over the past year. However—because my glass is always half full, usually with whisky—I look around and see that there are wonderful women out there doing the hard work of social justice.

They are the teenage girls in high schools fighting for the concept of "enthusiastic consent." The women who work every day in migrant communities, ensuring that the most marginalized members have access to legal rights. The women who run for office, even if they know their chances are slim. The women in tech who report their harassment, knowing they will be harassed once again for taking a stand.

In the following essays, I write about some of the women I've met over the years, who are doing vital work. I write about my own struggles to reconcile ambition and work and family and contentment, all against the backdrop of my own shocking tendency toward complete sloth.

When you read the essays that follow, I hope you manage to stay awake. I hope you laugh. I am honoured that you listen.

THE VOICE IN YOUR HEAD
IS AN ASSHOLE

THE VOICE IN your head is an asshole. Perhaps you already know this. Perhaps—although this is doubtful—the voice in your head echoes the voice in mine, and sounds like a whiny little bitch on Quaaludes.

The voice in your head would not want you to take Quaaludes, which are the drugs that hippies took to feel trippy and mellow. The voice in your head does not want you to be trippy or mellow. It does not want you to have a good time—ever. It does not want you to go out dancing in silver boots. It does not want you to wear that miniskirt once you're past the age of forty. It does not want you to go drinking with the college students you meet on the subway platform. It wants you to go home, right now, before you make a fool of yourself.

The voice in your head is an asshole. Above all else, it does not want you to test your wingspan. It does not want you to take the assignment from your boss, because it might end in tears or, worse, silence. It most certainly does not want you to take your boss's job. It does not want you to ask for a book contract, or go for an audition, or apply for a job promotion.

Why even apply for that promotion? asks the voice in your head. And maybe now the voice doesn't sound like a whiny little bitch because it's too clever for that. Now it sounds like Daniel Craig or James Mason or Patrick Stewart, some treacherous English bastard with a voice like liquid honey who is trying to seduce you into never leaving your room.

Look at the qualifications in that job description, says the voice in your head. You only have four of six. Do the math! Oh, that's right, you can't do the math. I made you drop math in grade 11. Still! You will be laughed out of the job interview. You will not even make it to the job interview, because the wise people on the selection committee did not make it past the first line of your CV, and are now convulsed in a heap, laughing at your ridiculous ambition. Aren't you glad? asks the voice in your head. Aren't you glad I saved you from that humiliation?

The voice in your head is an asshole, and I know this because the voice in my head is also an asshole. The voice in my head sometimes escapes its lead-lined box and slips out of my own mouth. And then I will hear myself saying "moron" or "dumbbell" out loud, and it is myself I'm addressing. Yes, the voice in my head has the vocabulary of a six-year-old—but the aim of an Olympic fencer.

I will find myself on the streetcar, lost in a reverie, and suddenly I will think of a foolish thing I've said to someone, or a sentence I could have written more sharply, or a question I asked that drew a frown, and the asshole in my head lets fly, and out it comes: "moron," I'll mutter to myself, sharply. "Idiot." People on the street-car turn to stare, and I purse my lips and look away and pretend that I was not calling myself names like a crazy person. It was the asshole in my head, I think.

One day I'll turn to the woman next to me and say, "It was just the voice in my head. It's an asshole."

And she will nod and say, "Mine, too."

They are cousins, our voices, or maybe frat broth-ers. They get together over a beer to talk about their triumphs.

The voice in your head is an asshole because it knows that it only has to spread the seed of doubt. It knows how fertile the soil already is. It knows the soil has been ploughed and enriched over the years by the teacher who said, *Hmmm, really,* and the friend who said, *Are you actually going out in that?* and the parent who said, *I just don't want you to be disappointed, honey.* That is some beautiful, dung-enriched soil! Along comes the voice in your head, sowing its toxic seeds, and is it any wonder they all take root?

If the voice in your head is a Grade A, world-class wanker like the voice in my head, it will tell you that what you want to do has already been done, and done better. It will tell you there is no point. It is not worth the grief. Someone better than you will do it better than you. It is safer here in the closet, under the bed, in the hamper under the dirty laundry. The seat at the head of the table is already taken. Moron, of course it's taken.

The voice in your head is an asshole, but it is also not very bright. You have this advantage. It can be caught, and put in a Tupperware, and placed on a shelf at the back of your mind, next to that guy you banged once in Acapulco and the curling lessons you never took, and all the other little regrets. It may rock and shake the Tupperware, but as long as you don't take pity on it and lift the lid to see how it's doing, it will stay contained indefinitely. It is a gremlin. It must never be fed.

If it escapes its Tupperware, it can be drowned out. The asshole has only one frequency, and you have an orchestra at your command. It can be drowned out by Nina Simone singing "Four Women" or PJ Harvey singing "Man-Size" or Beyoncé singing just about anything. The poetry of Emily Dickinson or Maya Angelou will rip that asshole's tongue right out of its mouth. If you laugh along to Wanda Sykes, it will shrivel up and die. The asshole's only strength is the strength it gains from shrieking, unmolested, in the echo chamber of your mind. It hates anything more interesting than itself; which is everything.

And, of course, you must have at least a sliver of sympathy for the voice, because its assholery is yours, its venom the awful seeping by-product of your insecurity. Your voice does not whisper alone. It is part of a magnificent chorale of self-denigration that women sing to themselves all over the world. There are people who do not have an asshole in their heads, who instead have a throaty-voiced cheerleader reclining on the chaise longue of their consciousness, saying, *Damn, they'd be lucky to have you for that job.* These people are called "men."

Take heart (as the asshole in your head shouts down your dreams) that it will tire eventually. It will age and grow weary before you do. And then it will slowly sputter and die, like HAL 9000 in the movie *2001: A Space Odyssey.* Remember when Dave the astronaut slowly dismantles HAL? HAL's voice, so sinister earlier in the movie, begins to fade as it pleads for its toxic existence:

"I can see you're really upset about this. I honestly think you ought to sit down calmly, take a stress pill, and think things over."

"I want to help you."

"I'm afraid, Dave."

This is the voice of inner assholes everywhere, as they lose the power to control. They will sputter out and die. Their songs will no longer seduce. Their insinuations will no longer strike fear. They will leave you in peace, by and large. You will be free to test your wingspan, unimpeded. Don't let it happen too late.

THE WAY OF THE HARASSER

IN HER WONDERFUL BOOK *Headscarves and Hymens: Why the Middle East Needs a Sexual Revolution*, the Egyptian-American feminist and journalist Mona Eltahawy writes about being assaulted in Mecca when she was a teenager—not once, but twice.

She was on the hajj, or pilgrimage, with her family. As she circled the Ka'aba, the stone sacred to Muslims, she felt a hand on her bottom: "I could not understand how, at this holiest of holy places, the place we all turned to when we prayed, someone could think to stick his hand on my ass and to keep it there till I managed to squirm away."

It got worse. When she joined a group of women ritually kissing the Ka'aba, the policeman who was supposed to be guarding the crowd reached out surreptitiously to touch her breast. She writes about her shock, as a fifteen-year-old who had never been touched in that way: "Surreptitiously: I came to learn during my years in Saudi Arabia and then in Egypt that this was how most men did it. That's how they got at your body—so surreptitiously that you ended up questioning your own sense of having been violated; your disgust at what had happened; whether, in fact, fingers actually did poke through the underside of your seat on a bus or ever so lightly brush against your ass as the man to which those fingers belonged looked the other way."

Eltahawy writes movingly about her struggles with wearing a headscarf, or hijab. Would "modesty" in clothing protect her from such unwanted attention? As her consciousness as a feminist grows, she realizes that there is no correlation between the way she is dressed and the groping to which she is constantly subjected. "If I were to use paint to indicate the places where my body was touched, groped or grabbed without my consent, even while wearing the hijab, my entire torso, back and front, would be covered with color."

She was in Jeddah and Cairo when she was assaulted. She could have been anywhere. She could have been any woman. I was certainly not wearing a hijab on a subway in Toronto one day when I was groped, though

I was wearing a singularly ugly sweatshirt that made people wonder if I were pregnant. It did not stop the guy walking down the stairs of the subway from reaching over, as casually as if he were waving hello, and cupping my breast. As if he were at home on the sofa stroking his balls, or his cat, or his Gameboy, or something else that belonged to him.

I say "the day I was groped," but, like every other woman I know, it was not one day, nor one quick feel. It has been, as Eltahawy says, a lifetime of being groped and leered at, of being shoved up against a wall, followed home, called a "bitch" for not smiling. I have never been to Jeddah or Cairo. These things happen in Toronto, in London, in Dublin, in New York, in Rome, in Vancouver.

That day in Toronto, I snapped. Perhaps I was hangry. Perhaps the subway was particularly rich with the smell of KFC and I was feeling faint. Perhaps I had had enough of men feeling that my body belonged to them, by benefit of being flaunted in public in its alluring grey fleece sack. I did something I have never done before or since to a groper: I turned and yelled, "Don't touch my tits, you asshole."

He kept walking. Of course he did! And thus I was the crazy lady in the subway, shouting at a phantom, while the polite people of Toronto averted their gazes and waited for the police to take me away.

As Eltahawy points out, street harassment is a global problem that is inflated to epidemic proportions in certain parts of the world. In Egypt, where sexual violence has been used by the state to suppress female dissidents (including Eltahawy herself), 99 percent of women and girls report experience with sexual harassment, according to the United Nations. It is a more grievous and pressing problem in certain parts of the world. But no matter where harassment occurs, and whether it is in a physical space or online, it has one purpose. And that purpose, as Eltawahy pithily observes, is "to remind us that public space is a male prerogative."

At what point do women realize they're not welcome in public places? The first time you feel a hand slip between your legs on the subway? The first time a guy calls you and your friend over to his car, as you're standing around talking about how cute Rob Lowe is, and rolls down the window to reveal his penis in his hand? The first time you walk through a dark parking lot with your car keys laced between your fingers?

Or is it later, when somebody with an egg for a face calls you a bitch on Twitter and informs you that he would rape you, but you're too ugly to be raped? Or when a gang of trolls descends to tell you just how stupid and wrong your views are, but then how would you know any better, feminazi? Or perhaps it's the first time a death threat arrives by email, with its extravagant misspellings and wonky capitalization.

The assault on women's autonomy — whether it happens on the street or online — is pervasive. It is crushing. It is an attempt to make us withdraw into ourselves, to retreat to a smaller space, to speak with a smaller voice. It has the effect of a No Girls Allowed sign on a boys' clubhouse door: Even as adult women, we are told there are places where we aren't welcome — or, if we are, it's as a collection of body parts.

Worse, it often happens in a way designed to make us question our own sanity. Did that really happen? That couldn't have just happened. This is known as "gaslighting," a term taken from the 1938 play and the famous film adapted from it. In the film, the nefarious Charles Boyer tries to drive his wife Ingrid Bergman slowly insane by insisting that the gaslights in their house aren't periodically dimming, though she can plainly see that they are (he's controlling the lights, of course, the bastard).

One evening many years ago, I was assigned to cover a tribute dinner for a high-profile Canadian author in a foreign city. At the pre-dinner reception, I clung to the life raft of a glass of white wine, and made conversation with people I'd never met before, as a reporter should. One man, a publishing executive, was particularly charming and solicitous. At dinner, I found myself sitting next to him, and I introduced myself to his wife, sitting on his other side.

The bread plate had barely had a chance to circulate before I felt his hand on my thigh. No, I thought. No way. I was there to write about the dinner; I had my notepad in front of me. I could have stabbed him with my pen. Instead, I shifted slightly away, which seemed guaranteed to end the episode without bloodshed. I felt his hand slide deeper, near my crotch. I looked over at his wife, who seemed oblivious. In fact, the groper seemed oblivious, too, his bland face concentrating on the speaker, as if his wandering hand was a creature entirely beyond his control. He was gaslighting me.

I had no idea what to do. What could I do? If it had happened later in my career, I probably would have leaned over and told the man that he was in danger of becoming the lede in my story. But I was young, and unsure, and the unreality of the moment had me doubting my own sanity. I slipped my hand under the table and pushed his away. He didn't flinch. He also didn't talk to me for the rest of the meal—which was a relief—nor did his tentacle slither toward my crotch again. He had had his jollies, a hot jolt of power over me.

When I read about harassment, in ensuing years, I would see this coal-black thread running through all the stories: The abuser thinks he can get away with it. It is impunity more than the promise of sex that gives him a thrill.

I went back to the hotel room that night and told the man I'd just started dating—who would become my husband—what had happened. He was shocked, and gently skeptical. That sounds terrible, but I was unsure at the time, too: Had it really happened? It was so implausible. Then I realized that my boyfriend was skeptical not because he didn't believe me, but because he had no frame of reference for this episode. No one had ever grabbed his crotch during an interview. No one had followed him home through dark streets, hissing all the way. No one had ever questioned his right to be human and unmolested in a public space.

Everywhere we go, women are made to feel less than human when we are out in the world. It is worse in some countries, as Mona Eltahawy writes, but no part of the globe is immune. Nor is the digital realm any safer for women: In some ways, the abuse there is even more pervasive.

Consider street harassment, which is the act of verbally or physically taunting a woman in public. According to a presentation by the UN Women's Safe Cities Initiative in 2015, it's a global phenomenon: 43 percent of women in London between the ages of eighteen and thirty-four said they'd experienced street harassment in the past year; in New Delhi, 92 percent of women reported being harassed; in Quito, 68 percent.

A 2014 study commissioned by the advocacy group Stop Street Harassment found that 65 percent of American women surveyed had experienced harassment, and nearly one-quarter of those (23 percent) had been sexually touched.

In 2015, the anti-harassment group Hollaback! released the results of a survey conducted in conjunction with Dr. Beth Livingston of Cornell University. More than 16,000 women in 22 countries were involved in the poll. More than 50 percent said they'd been groped or fondled; 71 percent said they'd been followed. Possibly the most disturbing finding was the age at which this harassment began: The majority of women reported that it began in puberty — when they were still girls. This is a wrenching lesson to learn, early on, about where you are allowed to be a free person.

Equally alarming was the fact that women around the world changed their behaviour as a way to avoid harassment. Eighty percent of respondents in India said they didn't like to go out at night, and the same number of women in South Africa said that being harassed made them change the way they dressed. Almost three-quarters of American women said they changed their method of transportation, and 79 percent of Canadian women surveyed said they'd been followed in the previous year.

The result of all this is a diminishment of women's lives, a shrinking of their sense of possibility and ambition. As the New Delhi–based women's rights group Jagori wrote in a report about building inclusive cities, "Insecurity and the threat and reality of violence prevent women and girls from participating as full and equal citizens in community life. Women and girls have a 'right to the city.'"

"A right to the city." You would think this would be self-evident, but the problem must be acknowledged before it can be addressed. The UN Women's Safe Cities Initiative works around the world to create urban spaces where women feel they belong: Kigali, Rwanda, began a program to educate taxi drivers and installed better street lighting; in Port Moresby, the capital of Papua New Guinea, where there was a high level of violence toward female vendors in the central marketplace, the market was redesigned with input from the women involved. In New Delhi, thousands of stickers were placed in rickshaws that said, "Sexual harassment is a crime, not a joke."

What if there's not even acknowledgement of the problem? In 2015, a video called "Ten Hours Walking as a Woman in New York City" set social media on fire, because ten hours walking boiled down to a lot of minutes being harassed. The video was commissioned by Hollaback! and featured a twenty-four-year-old actress named Shoshana Roberts walking through New York in jeans and a T-shirt, being filmed by a hidden GoPro. She was subject to more than a hundred comments, ranging from "How you doin'?" to "Hey, sexy" and "Hi, beautiful," to my favourite, "Somebody's acknowledging you for being beautiful. You should say thank you more!"

Ah, yes. Thank you for allowing me to be attractive enough to walk the streets of my city. Plain gals, follow me to the Ugly Women Tunnel. Please watch your head.

"Ten Hours Walking as a Woman" was an instant sensation and created mini-tornadoes of controversy: Was it racist to include so many Black and Latino men making comments? How was it offensive to say "Hello" or "How are you?" to a woman out walking? Was this not mere politeness? This argument is particularly evident in the comments on YouTube, where the video has been viewed 44 million times. What is she complaining about? These are "first world" problems.

Except, as we've seen, they're not. Around the world, men are incapable of allowing women an autonomous existence in a public space. Always, we have to be seen through the lens of male experience. Always we exist to be touched, commented on—and, if that fails, verbally assaulted—in ways men cannot possibly understand. Imagine a world in which men walk down the street in the morning, yelling "Smile!" at each other. I would pay to see that. I would watch a whole damn reality show involving nothing but men telling each other to smile.

I am old. Old in journalist years. Old if you count the rings on my liver. The harassment that happened to me on the street, which I've cited above, has died down. It is one of the great benefits of age: I no longer get chased, groped, whistled at, or told I'm an ungrateful bitch when I refuse to smile. Perhaps it's the glint off my fangs that scares them away.

But we don't just live in "meat space." We live, increasingly, online. It is the road we travel for work and pleasure. And that road is inhospitable to women. Too often it resembles a highway from *Mad Max: Fury Road*, with no Charlize Theron for badass relief. In the same way that we have been made unwelcome in public spaces, except as flesh, we are now told that we do not have a right to occupy what was once quaintly called the "information highway." There are signs, none of them subtle, indicating that we should exit as quickly as possible. This pervasive discrimination shows little sign of disappearing. We can try to ignore it or, pedal to the metal, smash this injustice flat and head for the open road.

ON A RAINY day in Toronto, I returned to the scene of some of my earliest crimes, Ryerson University. When I graduated with a journalism degree in 1988, it wasn't even a university; it was "a polytechnic institute," which in English means "a place to drink beer and nap for three years." In other words, I'm not even really a university graduate. Don't tell anyone.

I walked past a group of students lined up for free ice cream (some things never change) into Ryerson's journalism school, which is now part of the Faculty of Communication and Design (some things do change). The building smelled less like unwashed socks and despair than I remembered.

About half the folding chairs were empty for this panel discussion — "Hate, Trolls and Freedom of Expression Online: What to Do?" — hosted by Ryerson's Centre for Free Expression. The male guest was sick, so the panel consisted of two women who have been subject to online harassment, *Toronto Star* reporter Noor Javed and feminist activist Julie Lalonde, as well as Penni Stewart, an associate professor of sociology at York University. This was the second panel I'd been to in two weeks in which women described, in grotesque detail, the garbage hurled at them from the murky brown depths of the Internet.

I'm a newspaper columnist, so I recognized the outlines of the swamp and the toxic lumps that float in it. I take a fair amount of abuse — not as much as younger feminists, who seem to draw disproportionate ire, but enough that it causes steam to come out my ears. For example, in the brief lull between the two panels on cyber harassment, I found myself engaged in a Twitter debate with a gentleman who went by the name "Jalepeno Pooper" about whether I was as stupid as I appeared. This is not a debate I expected to have, at this stage in my career, with a man who cannot spell *jalapeño*. But there you have it: the modern world in all its glories.

The panel's moderator was Fuyuki Kurasawa, also from York's sociology faculty. He began by talking about the "digital injustice" that occurs when abusers drive their victims from social media: "Online abuse and online harassment create systematic barriers to participation. The members of groups disproportionately targeted by online hate and abuse are, and a lot of research demonstrates this, likely to withdraw from participation on social media platforms or modify the type of behaviour they engage in on social media, how they act, and what they say both online and offline."

In other words, the harassment ain't worth the harassment. It's bad enough being a woman on social media: try being a woman from an ethnic or religious minority, or LGBTQ. Try being a woman wearing a hijab. As Noor Javed said about her life as a reporter wearing a headscarf: "For years, anything I wrote would get hate mail. I was tired of it . . . I just wanted to go to work and not have people hating me just because I wore hijab, which is really what it sometimes comes down to."

All journalists are familiar with the dark byways of the digital utopia: The abuse that used to arrive in a stamped envelope, for your eyes only, is now spread like toxic waste across millions of pixels. For Javed, it was worse, as she and a colleague found out when they wrote a series of stories about a school principal who'd posted anti-Muslim opinions on a Facebook page. Javed's white colleague did not face any retaliation, but she did: "I started getting lots of online hate . . . There was an email smear campaign. There were libellous letters that went out calling me ISIS and Muslim Brotherhood."

Javed's colleagues and bosses and others in the online community stood up for her. She's a seasoned reporter, and not easily swayed, but even she felt the chilling effect of public abuse: "Hate has a toll on journalists, no question. It impacted me, it impacted editors dealing with me, it impacts what people want to write and say...If you're a young Muslim woman who's an intern, you don't even know if you should bring it up with your seniors."

For Julie Lalonde, an educator and advocate for victims of sexual and domestic violence, online threats and abuse are a daily constant. In 2014, Lalonde was conducting sex-assault education workshops at the Royal Military College in Kingston, Ontario, when she was subject to a torrent of abuse from the cadets she was supposed to be teaching: catcalls, laughter, taunting. Months later, the school apologized, but even that opened the floodgates of hate, and she was continually harassed via email and Twitter.

This drip-drip of misogyny would wear down the toughest stone. At the end of the panel, Lalonde said something that would become perhaps my favourite descriptor of the current digital landscape: "Online harassment is the equivalent of having a parrot on your shoulder who tells you you're a piece of shit 24/7." It made me laugh when she said it, but my laughter died pretty quickly. Then it made me want to hurl my laptop from the nearest bridge.

You only have to be a woman with an opinion and a wifi connection to understand precisely how annoying, damaging, and enraging it is to live in the digital age. Not all the time, of course, and not on all platforms. But for a not insignificant number of women—those who are doxxed (the public sharing of personal information), threatened with rape and dismemberment, told that they are grotesquely fat, ugly, and stupid, or that they're little better than animals—social media is a daily slog through a toxic swamp.

Female journalists know this. I write an opinion column and am told fairly regularly that I am, in the words of one of my gentleman callers, "a man-hating cunt." In the comments under my columns, I am regularly told that the sexism I am writing about does not exist and that I'm too stupid to know this. I have been told that I couldn't get a job working at one of Donald Trump's hotels because "Trump only has attractive people interacting with the public." Another of my pen pals wanted me to know that I am "too old for Trump to grope."

"Don't read the comments," journalists whisper to each other. If you're a female journalist, you might choose to do something more pleasant, like dig out your own liver with a rusty spoon. As the British journalist Helen Lewis has decreed in Lewis's Law: "The comments on any article about feminism justify feminism."

Dawn Foster, who moderated the comments section at the *Guardian* newspaper for two years, wrote about the nastiness of the experience: "The vast majority of commenters are men, and the *Guardian*'s own research shows that the writers most often abused on their site are women and Black journalists, and the least abused contributors—surprise—are white men." Many news organizations have abolished the comments, or drastically reshaped them to discourage cruelty. My own newspaper has implemented a "civil commenting platform" so that now that the threads are peppered with the phrase <this comment did not meet civility standards>. The phrase is everywhere through the comments, an eerie marker of past disease. You think, My God, what were they saying that's *worse* than what's on here now? And then you want to lie down, but you can't, because there are trolls to slay.

"What should I do?" young women journalists sometimes ask me, because as you get older you start to look like an oracle, especially in the cracked bits around the edges (unless you've had some work done, which of course I HAVE NOT). These young women are already exhausted: they're called "bitches" on Twitter, condescended to by male political journalists, savaged by drive-by assaults on Facebook. There is an oddly public nature to this abuse. I try to imagine a dentist happily drilling a tooth when a band of random nutcases breaks into her office and begins to scream, "Where did you learn to drill anyway, bitch? Where did you get your licence — the Whore School of Dentistry?"

You think I'm exaggerating, but it's so much worse than that. One of my newspaper colleagues told me that she had taken a dive into the comments on one of her stories — without a HazMat suit! — and found that one reader believed she was "only good for spreading her legs." It took two days for the comment to be removed.

The British activist Laura Bates set up the website Everyday Sexism as a repository for women's stories of mundane discrimination, only to be greeted on Twitter with "brutally graphic" rape threats. This was the moment, Bates writes, "that I became aware of the sheer force of hatred that greets women who speak out about sexism."

Sometimes the forces of hatred win, and we lose a valuable public voice. Consider the case of Lindy West, a whip-smart feminist and author of the hilarious essay collection *Shrill*. In early 2017, West announced that she would leave Twitter, not just because of the abuse she'd suffered, but because the platform had become a playground for the boy fascists of the alt-right. West wrote about her online battles:

I talk back and I am "feeding the trolls." I say nothing and the harassment escalates. I report threats and I am a "censor." I use mass-blocking tools to curb abuse and I am abused further for blocking "unfairly." I have to conclude, after half a decade of troubleshooting, that it may simply be impossible to make this platform usable for anyone but trolls, robots and dictators.

In 2016, the actress Leslie Jones was forced off Twitter by an organized campaign of racist, sexist abuse; trolls even impersonated her to make false homophobic attacks on other users. The only saving grace of that episode was the huge wave of support for Jones, which eventually led to her return to Twitter: "Welp…a bitch thought she could stay away. But who else is gonna live tweet Game of Thrones!!"

I am completely in sympathy with women who leave social media platforms; the energy required to joust online orcs could be better used for—well, just about anything, from making love to making blue Jell-O. Every time I see a sister leaving, though, I feel a pang of sorrow.

Because the point of this garbage landslide is to suffocate our voices. There is no other outcome that would make the goblins happier. They will dance around their midnight bonfires, clutching their Dorito bags, if they can force us to step away from our computers. If we can't be driven off the streets entirely, then they can at least drive us from the digital agora. And we can't let that happen.

The effort to address online misogyny will require a wide-reaching, coordinated response from powerful players within the digital realm. Social media platforms will need to do a better job of enforcing their codes of conduct; employers need to have solid anti-harassment policies to protect employees; police need to take threats seriously; schools need to enforce norms around cyberbullying.

In other words, don't hold your breath. So far, the efforts to address abuse have been weak and ineffectual. Presented with that (altogether unsurprising) leadership vacuum, warrior queens have stepped in to light the way. Mona Eltahawy, who I wrote about at the beginning of this chapter, likes to dismiss Twitter tormentors with the delectable phrase "Fuck off, kitten." Caitlin Moran, who likened the deterioration of Twitter to a "zoo set on fire," once led a two-day strike of Twitter to protest the misogyny that flooded the site.

When I interviewed Moran about her book *Moranifesto*, I asked what her solution would be for an online space that is welcoming to everyone — old and young, male and female, introvert and screamer. "I suspect we'll have to invent a new space," she said.

"And what would be great is if that was a space that was invented by women, for once, from the ground up. And it would be more like sitting around a dinner party talking, rather than someone coming through the door and firing off one-liners."

I asked if boys would be allowed.

"Absolutely," Moran said. "They'd just need to be told the rules."

Until this femtopia arrives, women will have to stick up for each other or risk being drowned separately in silence. This is already happening, in the most heartening ways, at ground level. Whether it translates into action, in a profit-driven digital landscape largely inhospitable to the female experience, is another matter.

Here's a story that begins in horror but ends in some hope. The British Labour MP Jess Phillips is an outspoken advocate for women's rights. "Gobby" is how such women are described in Britain. Sometimes it's even a compliment. But a gobby woman, especially one who speaks out in Parliament, is asking for a particular kind of muzzling. One day Phillips was wrapping her son's birthday presents when she was alerted to vicious online comments about a speech she had given in Parliament. She described the comments written by an anonymous citizen in her recent memoir, *Everywoman*: "You know what would be funny.

Pouring molten iron down this cunt's cunt till she starts vomiting bullets."

When she read that, Phillips burst into tears. Not because this kind of vitriol was new — in fact, she received threats, abuse, and insults about her appearance every day — but because she was, like so many women, tired of the fight: "I was just sick and angry at how acceptable it was to still hate women." Still, she knew precisely what her tormentors hoped: that she would shut up, shut down, go away. "The crux of why these people hate me is because I have a voice, and people listen to it. A woman with power is intolerable to them."

In her book, she begs young women not to give up. To refuse to be silenced. She encourages them to keep writing, and publishing, and sharing their opinions — which is, of course, their goddess-given right. It is easier said than done: Women of colour who are politicians are even more likely to be abused online than their white counterparts. In an Amnesty International survey of tweets sent to British members of parliament in the first six months of 2017, fully 45 percent of abusive tweets were sent to one person — Diane Abbott, a Black Labour MP. Female, Black, and Asian MPs received 35 percent more hateful messages than their white counterparts.

Instead of abandoning the digital ship, Phillips learned ways to steer her own course. She writes snarky retorts (this level of combativeness, she admits, is not for everyone). She asks for pictures of pets to be sent to her when she's going to be speaking on a subject that will draw the trolls, so that she sees something pleasant alongside the turds floating in her tweetstream.

Most importantly, she and other female politicians in the UK have formed a non-partisan alliance to stand up for each other online called Reclaim the Internet. The fact that she was flooded with thousands of rape threats the day after the initiative was announced is perhaps the best advertisement for its necessity (see Lewis's Law, page 36).

It's thrilling and uplifting to see women refuse to be driven away. Leslie Jones's return to Twitter was so triumphant and brash that her live-tweets of the Olympics earned her a job as an official commentator for NBC. Zoe Quinn, the game designer who was targeted and doxxed during the hateful Gamergate scandal, turned the tables by reclaiming the experience in a new memoir and by creating an advocacy group to help other women who are the victims of online harassment.

Quinn's memoir shares a title with the advocacy group she cofounded: Crash Override. The group's website offers a wide range of advice and protection for people who have been the victims of harassment. There's advice on protecting passwords, preventing doxxing, dealing with cops. The group's main advice, which I hope is some kind of balm to people who are being harassed, is: It's not your fault. It's never your fault.

Research shows that young women are disproportionately hassled online, whether it's the posting of "revenge porn" pictures or cyberstalking. LGBTQ women and women of colour are abused from every angle, and their struggle should be all of ours. Anyone can be targeted, though. Anyone can be threatened for the crime of being female and alive and free.

As women demand more space, the backlash will continue. Enemies of our freedom will attempt to drive us inside; enemies of our power will attempt to silence our voices. We can answer the threat any way we choose. We can answer the threat with more freedom.

FEARLESSNESS

ON THE MORNING of March 7, 2017, the expensively suited money lords arrived in lower Manhattan to find they had a guest. A little bronze guest called "Fearless Girl."

She stood about the height of an average ten-year-old, her feet planted firmly apart, her chin lifted in defiance, her hands planted on her hips. Her metal face wore a look of no-bull seriousness, which was useful since she was facing down a bull. Directly in front of Fearless Girl, across a couple of yards of the Bowling Green park, stood one of the most famous pieces of public art in New York, Charging Bull. Its horns were lowered, its front hoof raised in terrible readiness for the charge.

Fearless Girl had arrived on the morning before International Women's Day to face down the rampaging bull-god of American capitalism. Well, not really. Fearless Girl, it soon transpired, was not so much a critique of capitalism as a product of it. She was created by sculptor Kirsten Visbal at the behest of an investment firm called State Street Global Advisors and its advertising partner, McCann New York. State Street wanted to call attention to the lack of women in leadership roles in American corporate life; coincidentally, it had a gender-diversity investment fund just waiting for dollars to be pumped into it.

"Know the power of women in leadership," read a plaque planted near Fearless Girl's sensibly shod feet. The State Street logo was inscribed underneath.

Feminism has long been co-opted for capitalism's gain, but even by the standards of the game this was brazen cheek. The scent of hypocrisy was reminiscent of the product of the bull's back end.

"This statue...is an exercise in corporate imaging," wrote columnist Ginia Bellafante in the *New York Times*. "The point of 'Fearless Girl' was to advertise a State Street initiative pushing companies to include more women on their boards. Although the firm has said it is working to improve the number of female executives in its own ranks, it hasn't been close to exemplary in this regard: Of its 28-person leadership team, only five are women, according to the company website."

Despite this, Fearless Girl was an enormous hit from the moment she landed. Tourists lined up to take their pictures with her, copying her plucky stance. Parents brought their little girls to stand next to the statue, probably whispering exhortations of fearlessness into their ears. Instagram filled with photos. For $19.99, you could buy a T-shirt on Amazon that showed the girl and the bull, frozen in bronze showdown, next to the words "Be Fearless."

She proved so popular that she got invited to stay. Fearless Girl was supposed to stand for just a few weeks on Bowling Green, but New York Mayor Bill de Blasio announced that she would remain in place, drawing tourists and investors, for the next year, until International Women's Day 2018. In that time, she would remain a symbol of "standing up to fear, standing up to power, being able to find in yourself to do what's right." This was before the news arrived, in October 2017, that State Street would pay $5 million to settle a lawsuit brought by female employees who claimed they were paid less than men at the firm. Maybe they should have called our friend Fearlessly Asking for a Raise Girl.

I'm not sure that women need a bronze statue paid for by an investment firm planted in the money-mining centre of one of the world's richest cities to remind them to be brave. Women are brave, all over the world, every minute of every day, in far more challenging circumstances. Worse is the very idea of fearlessness: What a useless concept to drill into the heads of young women everywhere. No human being is without fear, except perhaps psychopaths and people high on acid, and neither of those should be taken as role models.

Run, I wanted to whisper to Fearless Girl every time I saw her picture posted on Facebook. *Run, plucky girl.* That's a goddamn charging bull, and you're armed with a ponytail. It's not a fair fight. Go home, read about how to take down a bull, and come back with a rifle or a lasso. "Gored Girl" isn't nearly as appealing as "Fearless Girl."

There is no shame in running, when running is what's called for. Standing your ground is the correct response in some situations, but sometimes you have to know when to live to fight another day. This is not a popular slogan for a T-shirt, nor will it receive many likes on Instagram. Instead, Instagram is filled with posts like this: "Once you become fearless life becomes limitless." Or, written in a bold cursive, "Be fearless in the pursuit of what sets your soul on fire."

Not just overcoming fear, but denying its existence: this is what young women are supposed to aspire to.

In 2012, the Women in the World Summit launched with the promise of "150 Fearless Women." Arianna Huffington, high priestess at the temple of earthly aspiration, wrote a book called *On Becoming Fearless: . . . In Love, Work and Life.* I considered writing a rebuttal called *Scared Shitless Most of the Time, Faking It the Rest*, but it seemed unlikely to be adapted for a Netflix series. I could "conquer my training regime" in Nike's Fearless Flyknit women's training shoe, were I not already afraid of running. Also, the shoe looks remarkably like the crocheted toilet-paper covers that my grandmother produced endlessly during my childhood. Now *those* were frightening.

Surely it's more useful to take the approach of Toronto media executive Denise Donlon, as reflected in the title of her memoir *Fearless as Possible (Under the Circumstances).* Because circumstance, and your neural network, will sometimes tell you that fear is precisely what you should be feeling at a particular moment. Fear, like pain, is one of nature's great red lights: Beware, all who pass this way. That's a tiger. That's a runaway train. That's a man who has no respect for your person. To suggest that young women should be fearless, that they should neither contain nor admit to fear, is to place yet another unattainable goal tantalizingly out of their reach. It becomes one more thin, painful switch for self-flagellation, more ammunition for the contemptuous inner critics. (See "The Voice in Your Head Is an Asshole," page 15.)

In the 2017 smash-hit live-action adaptation of *Beauty and the Beast*, Belle, played by Emma Watson, begs her father (Kevin Kline) to tell her something about her late mother. The father, his voice full of wonder, says, "Your mother was fearless. Fearless."

Was she, though? Or is he viewing her through the lens of his idealized love? Was she perhaps terrified much of the time, but unable to show it? Her clever and brave daughter, as we see in the course of the movie, is properly alarmed about things that are alarming: Belle is afraid that she'll lose her father, the one person she loves; she is afraid that she will have to give up her independence and marry the hulking meat-puppet, Gaston. The other villagers fear her because she is independent, unorthodox, and lettered; in return, she fears her estrangement from them. Belle is not fearless. Instead—and this is much more inspiring—she recognizes her fears and decides not to act on them. As a rational and resourceful young woman, she realizes her future depends on her not abandoning her soul to fear.

One of my favourite books of the past decade is Joanna Bourke's majestic *Fear: A Cultural History*. First, because it's fascinating. Second, because it is comforting.

The progression of terror throughout human history is humbling and puts our plight in perspective. Paleolithic man was afraid of fanged creatures, and drew pictures on the cave wall as a way of keeping those fears at bay; medieval peasant feared famine, and made obeisance to the church and king as a path to a full belly; a Victorian lady dreaded being buried alive (a surprisingly common fear), and asked that her throat be cut before she was boxed and placed in the grave. Historically, the extremely pious were often near-paralyzed with scrupulosity, "the fear of having sinned or offended God in some way." That is as incomprehensible to us as the fear of swiping right when we meant to swipe left would have been to them.

And what do we fear now, in a time when we have never been safer? We fear failure, and loss of status, and lingering death. Adolescent girls, famously, fear being humiliated in front of their peers, which is why girls' magazines are filled with deliciously cringey scenarios: "I tripped in front of my crush and the whole school LOLed!"

Bourke distinguishes between fear, the terror of something immediate and present, and anxiety, the swamp water of dread that creeps in at our ankles and rises higher till it drowns us in nameless, formless trepidation — of what? Something out there. We fear terrorism, when a North American is more likely to be killed by a fall in the bathtub than a terrorist's bomb, and ignore the threat of climate change, which will soon bake us like so many cookies forgotten in the oven.

Of course young women will fear, and should not be ashamed of it. The structures of the world were not built for their comfort. The law and economics are still tilted against them. Divorce is an economic bombshell. While young women shouldn't be consumed by fear, to suggest a hollow, macho posturing as a starting point does no one any good.

As Bourke points out, a little fear is more useful than its absence:

> A world without fear would be a dull world indeed... A world without fear would be a world without love. Fear has been one of the most significant driving forces in history, encouraging individuals to reflect more deeply and prompting them to action. Indeed, much of the human urge to creativity depends upon fear—fear of "being struck down in our prime," of being rejected, of not understanding how one's lover will respond and of self-consciousness.

To elevate fearlessness as moral exemplar, to suggest a girl bursts into the world with a Ronda Rousey kick to the head, is to lose the humanity of fear's progression throughout a lifetime. That is, the terrors that plague you at twelve, or seventeen, or twenty-eight, are entirely different from the ones that wake you up at forty-five, in the hour of the wolf, the darkest part of the night, while your partner snores blithely beside you. A life can be traced in the evolution of its anxieties: the ones overcome, the ones shelved, the ones that remain monsters always, never fully caged or killed.

I am, for example, quite shocked when I look back on my childhood fears. I was claustrophobic. Spiders sent me running. For years I had suffered an irrational, panicky terror that a nuclear war would break out, shattering my glasses—the precise sequence of events was unclear—and then, rendered near-blind and useless, I'd be abandoned and left for dead.

Once, I was terrified of public speaking: The very thought made my bladder ache. Silent screams filled my head for weeks before I had to give a speech, or moderate a panel, or interview someone on stage. Slowly I learned that the way to cope with the fear was a) to over-prepare, and b) to recognize that the consequences of even a failed public appearance were not very dire after all. Perhaps people would yawn. Perhaps they wouldn't laugh. These things were temporarily painful but inconsequential in the long run. Now I'm terrified of driving on the highway: This is not a fear I can talk myself out of, using the above method. What's the worst thing that could happen on a highway? Oh yes, fiery death. Limbs strewn across the asphalt. I'm still working my way through that one.

Age alters our fears even as it alters our bodies. I'm no longer afraid of public speaking, but I also have no strength in my pelvic floor. I don't pee myself out of fear; I just pee myself. This is what is known in middle age as "a fair trade-off."

From this vantage, I sometimes look back on the macho idiot I once was. I think about the men I drunkenly went home with, not knowing their names and barely remembering my own, fully trusting my ability to get out of any situation, no matter how sticky.

One morning many years ago, I woke to the sound of the phone ringing in the apartment I shared with two friends. The phone frequently failed to work because it was sodden with beer or, if we were flush, vodka. But on this morning it functioned. My roommate was on the other end, hungover and confused.

I'd last seen her in the bar the night before. Vaguely, I remembered that she'd left with a man she'd just met. He had been wearing gold slippers, which for my friend was the mating equivalent of a peacock's spread tail. Now she was awake, with no money and no memory of how she'd arrived wherever she was. Gold slipper man snored on, oblivious.

"I have no idea where I am," she whispered.

"Go and look out the window," I said. "Look for a street sign."

She put down the phone and came back a minute later, hysterical with giggles: "I can't see any street signs. But I do have my eye on the gold slippers."

It turned out all right in the end: She's still alive, and still one of my best friends. But the thought of it now makes my heart clench. The thought of my daughter, being so careless, so fearless, fills me with a dread I can't name. I shake my head to remove even the picture of it. (You notice I don't worry about my son being spirited away to a stranger's apartment. My conditioning is strong. My fears for him are completely different, and equally seismic.)

Obviously, I don't walk around in a constant state of panic, or I would need a Costco-sized bottle of Valium to get me through the day, but there is a steady hum of anxiety for my children at the back of my brain. I worry that robots will take their jobs. I worry that a plague will take their health. I worry that they will not find comfort, or peace, or the love that I have with their father.

This business of living takes effort. It takes resourcefulness. And sometimes it will be terrifying. To pretend otherwise, to glibly pretend fearlessness, is to provide platitudes where tools should be. Fear can provide a light. It should not be everything; that would be a paralyzed life. But it's not nothing, either. It exists, we live with it, and we can bend it to our will.

WEDDINGS ARE SATAN'S PLAYGROUND: A LETTER TO MY DAUGHTER

Dear Maud,

My most cherished hope for you and your brother is that you will each find someone to love, and be loved by that person in return. Otherwise, your ambitions are your own to determine. Take care of your heart, and the rest will follow.

Once, when you were four years old, you were playing with your friend Martha at our house in London, and the two of you came up to me, holding hands. You tugged my sleeve.

"Mum?"

"Yes?"

You looked at Martha, who was, if I remember correctly, eating a Jammy Dodger. "Mans can marry mans, right?"

I debated whether to get into the whole question of global human rights, but settled for a local answer: "Yes, they can."

"And ladies can marry ladies?"

"Absolutely."

You looked over at Martha again, clearly imagining your future nuptials, the two of you dressed in matching Peppa Pig gowns. You looked puzzled. Finally, you said, "Then why did you marry Dad?"

I immediately went to tell your father that story, of course. I hope to be telling that story forever, unless you tell me it's too embarrassing, in which case — sorry, too late. There's only one place I hope not to tell that story, and that's at your wedding, because I hope you don't have one. At least not a traditional one, where the bride is received as if she has won the greatest of life's prizes: a man to marry. I mean, get married if you want — I did. Be joyful and bountiful in your love. Have a party, dance, laugh. But don't feel you have to engage in the Olympics of one-upmanship that is the modern wedding.

I know, it may seem slightly hypocritical, given

the amount of wedding-related television we watch. There's *Four Weddings* and *Say Yes to the Dress* and those artificial twin peaks of showmance, *The Bachelor* and *The Bachelorette*. But I feel that each episode is actually a tiny vaccine against the virus. We lie sprawled on the couch in the basement watching four women compete to see whose wedding deserves the free honeymoon—the lady who got married in the shark tank? the woman who made all the food for two hundred guests?—and I feel that I'm ensuring your shots are up to date.

We watch *Say Yes to the Dress* and recoil in horror and delight at the bridal shoppers at Kleinfeld, as family dysfunction unspools against a backdrop of satin fit-and-flares and $20,000 princess ball gowns containing more crystals than an entire chorus line at the Bellagio. "Not enough bling," whispers the bride, crushed. "It makes you look like a linebacker," says a sister, mining a vein of sibling resentment that lies an inch below the surface. And I look at you, Maud, and think, Please, let's never do this. Please have a paintball wedding instead.

And as we watch, I will point out to you that these shows—like commercials for laundry detergent or diet products—present a world almost entirely free of men. The wedding, and by extension the marriage, is seen as women's work. Only she would be invested in the emotional labour of making sure the day is perfect, in its million expensive details, from the cake to the photographs. She is the successful hunter, and he is dragged, like a shot deer, from one ridiculous appointment to the next. Occasionally he is prodded to life so that he can mumble, "Sure, honey, teal works for me."

But there is one universe where the men are equally involved, isn't there? We watch far too much of *The Bachelor*, in which dozens of women with the finest hair and bodies that science can produce compete for the attention of one man. Its sister show, *The Bachelorette*, reverses the genders. Both shows are draped in the filmiest of modern camouflage but might as well take place five hundred years ago, lit by the flicker of a tallow candle: There is always the expectation of a proposal at the end, and it is always—always—the man who proposes. But she is the victor; the ring the spoils.

Okay, I'm being a bit hard on *The Bachelor*. It's been fun and educational for the whole family, hasn't it? Remember when we tried to make Granny watch an episode, and she looked at the bachelor—his teeth much brighter than his eyes—and said, "Do you think he has all his wits about him?"

At every opportunity, I've outsourced life lessons to *The Bachelor*. There was the time when I used the Fantasy Suite episode to explain human reproduction, and you turned to me and rolled your eyes and said,

"I know how it works." I know, I'm terrible. I fully expected Children's Aid to show up and take you and your brother away.

You'll notice I'm not addressing this letter to your brother, by the way. That's because society has broader and more interesting ambitions for him than the precise shade of pewter in the centrepiece or whether St. Bart's is the hottest spot for a destination wedding. Perhaps I am unwittingly feeding into the stereotype as well when we watch these shows together.

But then, life is full of contradiction and complexity. You will find this out. You're probably already starting to discover it. For example, you may point out that Dad and I got married, and made our peace with societal convention. And that is true. Except that none of it was conventional, and the only place our wedding would have been featured is Ripley's Believe It or Not!

I could have proposed, like a good feminist, but I didn't. Dad proposed, if you can call it that, as we were driving back from IKEA in our decrepit K-car, which leaked fuel and stalled during left turns.

"Maybe we should get married," he said, startling me from my reverie about whether I should wash my hair for the first time that week.

"Sure," I said. Or possibly "Okay" or "Why not?"

We both thought of ourselves as beatniks at heart.

Even if we'd had the money—which we didn't—our wedding would never have been about floral arrangements and flung garters. I'd been to too many that were joyless and artificial, the bride and the groom stressed and weary. I'd watched how weddings had become a status trap, a retrograde game show. Imagine being handed over from one man to another!

So we eloped instead. I wore a tiny red mini dress covered with Eiffel Towers. We got married on the site of an ancient fort in Nova Scotia, in the town where your great-grandparents are buried. The justice of the peace was not used to tiny, reckless weddings. She said, "Are you sure you want to get married outside? It's twenty bucks extra." The fellow who was supposed to be our best man couldn't make it because he was planting turnips that day—a true story, ask your dad—so his name had to be covered with Wite-Out on our marriage certificate. Maybe that makes it invalid. Who cares? Your dad's name is written on my heart. (Are you throwing up yet?)

The whole thing cost a couple hundred dollars. It left us enough money to throw a party for our friends in Toronto, where we danced to our first song, the dancehall classic "Murder She Wrote." Do you know how much an average Canadian wedding costs these days, Maud? It's $27,000. You could travel around the world for that amount of money. You could buy a racehorse!

I hope it doesn't shock you to hear this, but your dad was not the first man I'd, um, "dated." Nor was I the first woman for him, though I was certainly the first woman he'd proposed to in a car that was little better than a barbeque on wheels. We'd both been around the block. When we found each other, we were busy doing other things — working, travelling, and in your dad's case inventing a new cocktail called the "Braino" (equal parts Pernod and Brio, it should have made him famous).

My point is that neither one of us was consumed with the idea of "the one." The idea of "the one" is a pernicious myth propagated by Disney and *The Bachelor*, which, now that I think of it, belong to the same corporate empire. You notice how few of the matches on *The Bachelor* ended up lasting? I rest my case. There is no "one," there are many — many people with whom you could share a happy life. Or your happy life may involve a series of matches, which worked for Elizabeth Taylor. Or it may be that your happy life involves you, alone, with a lot of cats. I think that's your plan at this point, though it may change.

Anyway, sweetheart, you will make this decision for yourself. You may choose never to marry. You may choose to live in a commune, or on a mountaintop with goats. Or perhaps you will choose to have a lavish, splendid wedding with a white dress and live peacocks and a samba band. I doubt it, because it doesn't seem like you, but I have no way of seeing into the future. And if that is what you choose, I will be with you every step of the way. And I will never, not once, tell you that your dress makes you look like a linebacker.

Your loving Mum

AMBITION: THREE LIFE LESSONS

AT THE AGE of fifteen, I went with my friend Bonnie to
see a movie that would change the way I thought about
my future. The film remains my favourite to this day,
a bright and flickering constant when my life shifted
in ways I couldn't have imagined.

Bonnie was a decade older than me. She existed on
a plane of impossible sophistication, living in an apartment on College Street and making black bean soup
that she served in hollowed-out pumpernickel loaves.
She was sardonic, cool-eyed, ardently feminist. We
worked together at the Eglinton movie theatre, where
every night, dressed in brown polyester uniforms
reeking of old butter, we would mouth the dialogue
to *Octopussy* as we cleaned the popcorn machine.

One night Bonnie took me to a repertory cinema to see *My Brilliant Career*, an Australian movie directed by Gillian Armstrong that had been released a few years earlier, in 1979. Rep cinema! Foreign film! These were gateways to adulthood, and I worshipped Bonnie for taking my yearning seriously. I watched it open-mouthed, tiny explosions going off in my brain. It was a movie set near the beginning of the twentieth century, in rural Australia, but every line of dialogue could have come from my own journal, with its pages alternately tear-stained and hunger-filled.

"Bad enough to be born a girl," says the main character, Sybylla Melvyn. "But to be born ugly and clever!" Sybylla, played by the inimitable Judy Davis, wants something *more* from life. The ambitious daughter of a dirt-poor farm family, she reads to her grubby siblings from the pages of novels that paper the walls of their shack. She is fierce and rebellious, mischievous and prickly. (The film is based on a famous 1901 Australian novel written by a sixteen-year-old girl called Miles Franklin, who would become an influential feminist and writer, though she never recaptured the success of her first book.)

Prickly doesn't work for girls, not even in the bush. Sybylla must be made smooth, her ambition sanded down. To that end, she is sent to live with her rich grandmother, who will tame her wild hair and spirit, in preparation for marriage. But Sybylla does not want to be married.

"I'm going to have a career," she announces to her grandmother, who nearly expires of shock.

"A career," intones the grandmother, deadly quiet. "What in?"

"I don't know," says Sybylla blithely. "Literature, music, art. Maybe the opera! I haven't made my mind up yet."

The grandmother glides away, to seek smelling salts, perhaps, or a knife.

There is a complicating factor, a spanner in the works of Sybylla's ambition. A local landowner's son, Harry Beecham (played by delectable young Sam Neill), has fallen in love with her. Unfortunately for Harry, Sybylla's heart longs for the world more than it lusts for him. In a truly heart-wrenching scene, she tells him that her ambition will crush him if they remain together, and she leaves. We see her, at the end of the film, sending the manuscript of her novel off to a publisher in Sydney.

"But why," I said to Bonnie, as we left the theatre. "Why couldn't she have both?" I was alight with thoughts and feelings. Like Sybylla, I burned to do something in the world, though I wasn't sure what.

Would my ambition crush or liberate me? Why could Sybylla not desire worldly success *and* Harry? Sam Neill had ignited my teenaged hormones. I couldn't imagine anyone abandoning him for a pen and inkpot.

Bonnie sighed, exhaling the *Weltschmerz* of her twenty-five years. "It's harder for women," she said. "The world is afraid of what we want."

The world is afraid of what we want. Why wasn't the world afraid of what men wanted? I refused to live with such a double standard. I would write books and have a husband, I told Bonnie, or possibly just many, many lovers, all of whom looked like Sam Neill and brought me coffee while I typed, before reading my pages and marvelling at my genius.

Soon after Bonnie and I went to see *My Brilliant Career*, I bought a copy of the movie on vhs and played it to wheezy death. Then I bought it on DVD, and its rainbow surface became marred with fingerprints and spilled drinks. Finally, I watched it on YouTube, for free. Technology expanded, but the world did not progress alongside it: Sybylla's struggle to reconcile her inside and her outside, to maintain her essential Sybylla-ness while doling out pieces of herself to the world, is still the struggle of women today. Our ambition remains a minefield. The world is afraid of what we want. Or perhaps we are afraid of what we want.

It's possible, at this moment, that we're even slipping backward when we consider the full potential of women's lives. Early in 2017, social-science data from the United States showed an alarming trend toward millennials favouring a retrograde vision of a domestic partnership, with the man providing the main income support in a partnership and the woman working inside the home. In a survey of high-school students, the Council on Contemporary Families revealed that 58 percent of high-school seniors preferred that "traditional" model; twenty years before, only 42 percent of seniors favoured the male breadwinner model.

As the *New York Times* reported, looking at related studies around millennials' attitudes: "Overall, Americans aged 18–34 are less comfortable than their elders with the idea of women holding roles historically held by men. And millennial men are significantly more likely than Gen X or Boomer men to say that society has already made all the changes necessary to create equality in the workplace."

Another academic study from 2017, "Acting Wife: Marriage Market Incentives and Labour Market Investments," demonstrates how even highly educated young women will lessen the scope of their professional ambitions when in the presence of dateable men. Not for their own sake, but because men find their ambition frightening. As the study's authors write: "Even in the 21st century, men prefer female partners who are less professionally ambitious than they are...Men tend to avoid female partners with characteristics usually associated with professional ambition, such as high levels of education."

In the study of female MBA students, those who were single were found to have participated less often in class and to have asked for raises less often. In a questionnaire outlining their professional goals, they were more likely to say they'd work harder and travel more if they knew the questionnaires wouldn't be shared among their classmates. In other words, they wanted to look less ambitious among men they might want to have relationships with.

If you asked those MBA students the same question at a different point in their careers, you'd probably get a different answer. Our ambitions ebb and flow with the years. They expand and contract to fit the contours of our fluid lives. The size and scope of these ambitions will depend on how supportive our work environments and social networks are. The very nature of the things we want to achieve will likely change. I didn't know any of that when I was fifteen.

All I ever wanted to do was to write a book. I didn't publish one until I was forty-seven. What was I doing in those intervening years? Shooting two babies out of my birth canal, for starters. I was working as a journalist. Chasing the wrong men. Drinking. Idling. Being productive and being fallow. Climbing ladders, descending ladders, choosing different ladders. Living in three different countries.

I've been fortunate enough to reach the age of fifty, which means I've had a lot of time to think about ambition, mine and other women's. It is a topic as vast and deep as the ocean. You can really only understand the patch you're currently sailing in and the bits you've made it through, sometimes with your sails tightly furled, sometimes with them gloriously open to the winds. It is almost impossible to chart someone else's path. All I can share with you are the three lessons I learned along the way.

THE PATH DOESN'T GO STRAIGHT UPWARDS

I said yes to the first book contract that I was offered, and immediately regretted it. That was in early 2001, when a publisher wanted me to write a book about bad girls in history. I was excited. As I talked with the editor on the phone, pacing my balcony in Los Angeles, I contemplated my empty work life suddenly filling with research about Lucrezia Borgia's taste in poison.

I hung up and was overcome by terror: Who was I to write a book? Where would I even begin? I envisaged, years down the road, savage reviews in newspapers. The asshole voice in my head was on his game that day.

Shortly after, I discovered I was pregnant. I begged off the book project with a shameful sense of relief. Now I wouldn't have to write the book, which meant I wouldn't have to be found out as a fraudster of the highest order. My unborn son became an excuse to turn the world away.

I lay awake at night, thinking of the telegram that the great screenwriter Henry Mankiewicz had sent to his friend Ben Hecht in 1925, urging him to move to LA: "Millions are to be grabbed out here, and your only competition is idiots." From the window by my bed, on a clear day, I could see the Hollywood sign in the distance, as tiny as the last line on an eye doctor's chart. In 1932, the starlet Peg Entwistle had hurled herself from the *H* in a fit of despair over her floundering career.

Los Angeles is a city built of ambition, the way other cities are built of bricks. Everywhere I went, people burned for success: Our cat-sitter was a strip-club DJ who longed to be a famous musician; our building superintendent never doubted that his destiny lay in hip-hop greatness; a budding filmmaker dragged me onto the beach at Santa Monica to be part of his *Apocalypse Now* re-enactment.

Other women would have written the book while pregnant, finishing the last edits as the C-section scalpel descended. I was not other women. I felt tremendous guilt at my own lack of reach, shame at my failure to take all that was offered. Wasn't I supposed to reach higher, and higher? Professionally, I had climbed with determination since I left journalism school at the age of twenty-one: By twenty-four, I was the books editor of Canada's national newspaper; by thirty-two, I was second-in-command of a national woman's magazine.

What a self-satisfied idiot I was. The ladder did not work that way. I climbed a few rungs, and found the next one was rotted. Or I climbed behind my husband for a few years, because his ladder was sturdier. Sometimes there were snakes instead of ladders, and I tumbled downward quickly, my hands grasping for purchase.

Later, when we were living in London with a second baby, my neighbour Jo would describe the in/out predicament better than I ever could. Jo was a barrister who also had a doctorate in history from Oxford. She slacked not. Yet she, too, felt the terrible pull of the current, dragging her toward home, dragging her away again. When her third child was born, she asked to work part-time at the law firm, and ended up irritated and unfulfilled whether she was at home or at the office: "I resent them when they ask me to do something," she said, as we stood in her garden watching our children play, "and I resent them when they pass me over and give the work to someone else."

YOU'RE NOT THE PROBLEM. YOUR OFFICE IS.

Too often the issue of ambition is framed as a personal one. (I've done it here, in this essay.) The truth is, women's ambitions are constrained by systemic forces beyond our control. They include, but are not limited to, inherent biases that favour the promotion of people already in power, that is, non-racialized men; lack of access to affordable child care; inflexible managerial systems that do not encourage different modes of working; and lack of professional networks that would aid women's ascent to power.

I was a mossy old river stone before I realized any of these things, despite the fact that I'd written about the exclusionary aspects of male power dominance for decades. I knew about the paucity of women in boardrooms, which my newspaper colleagues wrote about every year. (In Canada, women fill 12 percent of the seats on corporate boards, and 45 percent of boards contain no women at all. While I was writing this book, a non-profit group that aims to promote women in the workplace, Catalyst Canada, named the new chair of its advisory board. They chose a man. He was the second man in a row to fill that role.) I could see the repressive power structures that kept us out of the corner office, but when I looked at my own career trajectory, I saw it through the lens of my own personal strengths and weaknesses, and not as part of a larger framework constructed by forces beyond my control.

After we returned from Los Angeles, I was hired as a section editor in my old newsroom, a management position. I had a tiny, windowless office and twenty-eight people reporting to me, which is about twenty-four more than you're supposed to have, according to the best practices of middle management. Not that I knew anything about middle management; the entire culture of the newspaper, at least then, was: learn on the job, sink or swim, and other fairly useless mottos that could be embroidered on a pillow.

I was not a very good manager. I absorbed people's pain like a sponge, and there was, for whatever reason, a great deal of pain to be absorbed. "Your department's a fucking casualty ward," one of the other managers said, with what seemed suspiciously like glee. One day, after a particularly harrowing week in which several people cried in my office, a journalist sat down across from me and burst into tears. I rummaged around in my desk for Kleenex but found they'd all been used to mop up other tears. All I had left were black cocktail napkins. I handed him one and watched, horrified, as it collapsed under the weight of his tears and left tiny black streaks on his cheeks. As I say: inexperienced manager. With better training—with any training—I might have learned to deflect the collective pain of my department and channelled it toward something more useful.

But I did not have more experience, and there was no one to train me, except my beloved mentor, who sat in the office next to mine and kept me sane. Once, and only once, we were sent on a day-long management training seminar. There was nothing she could do about the culture of bias inherent in the newsroom, though. Newsrooms are notoriously conservative places: We are very good at writing about change and very bad at implementing it. There was an atmosphere of sexism baked into the place, which we collectively agreed to ignore, much as we ignored the dirt embedded in the decades-old carpets.

There was an older guy I had worked with when I first came to the newspaper who resented having me as a boss. Our struggles came to a head and resulted in a meeting where both the union and Human Resources were present. This man had been waiting for his moment to dig the knife in: "I know you're young and in over your head," he said, with mock sympathy. "I'm sure you're doing your best."

He was an anomaly. The majority of people in the department were smart, resourceful, hard-working, and kind enough to keep any resentment they felt under wraps. It wasn't the people below me in the management structure who were the problem.

One day, at the morning news meeting where the next day's paper is mapped, a senior editor—who outranked me in the power structure—noticed the red boots I was wearing.

"Cool boots," he said.

"Thanks. They're new."

"You should show everyone."

I sat up and stared at him. "What?"

"Put them on the table," he said. "Show everyone your boots."

The rest of the managers looked at us blankly, eager to get back to their coffee and cigarettes and deadlines.

I shook my head, no. I couldn't believe this was happening.

"C'mon," the senior editor said, in a tone that implied *I'm just joking, can't you take a joke?* "Show everyone your boots."

He was not about to let it go. Slowly I put one boot on the table, feeling enraged and humiliated. There were only a couple of other women managers in the room, but they looked away, mortified. The men shuffled their schedules. I put my foot away, boiling with rage, unable to say anything. I should have said something. It was my Norma Rae moment. I could have scrawled "sexism" on a piece of paper and held it up; I could have taken him aside after. I didn't.

There were few women in upper management at my newspaper. There has never, for example, been a female editor-in-chief or publisher. My former colleague Vivian Smith has written an entire book about the way that my beloved profession is hostile to the ambitions of half its workforce. Her research is collected in her 2015 book called *Outsiders Still: Why Women Journalists Love and Leave Their Newspaper Careers*. The journalists she interviewed experienced much the same thing I had—casual sexism, ingrained networks that enforced existing power structures, a macho adherence to punishing hours and schedules. It is a workplace, Smith writes, "that has been hostile to women for 150 years."

Newspapers are not alone in failing to nourish women's ambitions or to provide a pathway to upward mobility. A fascinating report from Boston Consulting in 2017 offered a glimpse into why and how women advance in workplaces. It revealed that personal ambition does not die with age or when a woman chooses to have children, but is smothered by workplaces that do not actively promote gender equity. In other words, it's not us, it's them.

Boston Consulting surveyed 200,000 women, and the results showed that "women start their careers with just as much ambition as men. Women's ambitions do vary, but they vary by company, not by family status. When companies create a positive culture and attitude regarding gender diversity, all women—mothers included—are eager to advance."

This conundrum—female ambition ground down in the jaws of an unforgiving workplace culture—was brought into the spotlight a few years ago when one very high-profile woman decided to write about it. In July 2012, Anne-Marie Slaughter wrote a piece for *The Atlantic* about her struggles to balance her career as first female policy director for the U.S. State Department with her guilt over being absent in the lives of her sons, one of whom was struggling in the mire of adolescence. It was titled "Why Women Still Can't Have It All," and it set off an explosion in the fireworks factory of our worldly ambitions.

Slaughter's arguments, later expanded into the book *Unfinished Business: Women Men Work Family,* were nuanced and complex: She acknowledged that she was writing from a position of material privilege, which many women didn't share, and that the real problems with women gaining traction in the world were systemic, and not individual. It was the office that was fucked, and not the drones who toiled in it. As she wrote: "The culture of 'time macho' — a relentless competition to work harder, stay later, pull more all-nighters, travel around the world and bill the extra hours that the international date line affords you — remains astonishingly prevalent among professionals today."

People's well-being will improve and become more humane, she argued, only when the leadership gap closes, which would require her country "to elect a woman president and 50 women senators; to ensure that women are equally represented in the ranks of corporate executives and judicial leaders. Only when women wield power in sufficient numbers will we create a society that genuinely works for all women. That will be a society that works for everyone."

As for me, I was exhausted and dispirited after two years in management. When my husband was offered the job of European bureau chief for our newspaper, based in London, I jumped at the chance to accompany him. There, I would go back to being a regular old reporter, no longer burdened with having to worry about anyone's neuroses or career path but my own.

YOU JUST MIGHT FIND YOU'LL GET WHAT YOU NEED

Here is something that took me years to learn, and I share it now in the hopes that it may stick a few pins in your own voodoo doll of anxiety: Ambition, in our late-capitalist world, is almost entirely expressed in terms of work. That is, in terms of the labour you sell to your employer, or which you sell on the open marketplace. This is a monstrously constricted view of human potential. For too long, when we talk about women's dreams made manifest, we talk about jobs versus our families. The "all" in "having it all" is an office and a house filled with children. It does not consider the totality of women's lives, the huge space of creativity and fulfillment to be found outside those fenced areas.

What if your ambition instead is to be an extra-ordinary volunteer at the local old-age home, and that's where you find your deepest satisfaction? What if you dream of making the world's best paella? What if you want to be a foster mom to possums? What if you come most alive when you're neither a worker nor a mother, but a chorister, a woodworker, a surfer? What if the greatest satisfaction you ever feel comes in looking after an elderly parent? Why are these things not considered important peaks in the mountain range of our ambition?

For some women, ambition will rest primarily in the realm of career, whatever that career may be. Everything possible must be done to support that choice. I have certainly found an extraordinary home for my energies in daily journalism, and was lucky enough to be among the last dinosaurs walking Planet Newspaper. But we now place a debilitating burden on the workplace (and its attendant status and monetary rewards) as the entire repository of our dreams.

It's scary to step off the professional carousel, however briefly, and to know that it will not slow down for your return. If you're lucky, when you decide to return you'll leap back on, catching the tail of a pink unicorn while your briefcase bursts open and spews diapers and Advil and spreadsheets to the wind.

I stepped off the carousel. My daughter, our second child, was a year old, and I'd had my allotted year of maternity leave. I asked my newspaper if I could work three days a week. My editors agreed. It was a sacrifice for our finances, but it made sense, as it does in any household where two large careers collide with two small children.

My husband was away reporting half the time, and I told myself that I was doing what was right for the children—and, crucially, for me. I could not slice the pie of myself any more thinly and still feed everyone. I wanted my life to be different, and wider, and more creative. I wanted to write that book.

I still felt a pang of guilt every time I turned down a magazine assignment or opened a chiding email from an editor. I was envious when I saw colleagues take on glamorous assignments. But I placed the envy and the guilt in the same mental Tupperware where I stored my inner asshole voice, the one that told me my work was fruitless, and I sat down to write.

I worked on my novel while my kids were at school during those two days a week. Three years later, I had a book. Many drafts later, I had a finished book. Many rejection slips later, I had a publisher. I became Sybylla Melvyn on the day I found out I would be a published author. All my prickly bits were still in place, all my rough parts unsanded. And it was fine that way.

For years before and after I wrote my first novel, I interviewed other women about their ambitions, and I realized that each story was different and too oddly shaped to fit into a convenient narrative. Each path was different—not better, or happier, or more frustrating, just different. There was no point in looking at anyone else's map and wishing I were there. I was where I was, and I could be somewhere else tomorrow.

YOU'LL PAY FOR THOSE BREASTS,
OR THE COST OF BEING A LADY

I WAS THIRTEEN and in grade 8 when my classmate Oliver slipped his hand up my back, under my grey velour cowl-neck, and flicked my bra strap. He did it with the facility of one of Henry V's archers, tugging adroitly and releasing, as if our middle school were Agincourt and the French were in his sights.

"I like you, Renzetti," he said. "You're smart, and you've got big tits."

Both of these things were true, and would continue to be true, and would hang in the balance — if you'll pardon the pun — for the rest of my life. It was a combination that confused people. It confused me. Having big tits, for no reason that I could discern at that point in my youth, meant that you were somehow mentally deficient, as if brain matter had been redistributed south to build a bigger pair. Barbie had huge breasts and thought math was hard; Jayne Mansfield was seldom called upon to do quadratic equations. All the little-tittied girls were clever, sleek, unburdened by expectation. Another reason to be jealous of them: Over the course of a lifetime, they would not have to spend the equivalent of a luxury vacation corralling their breasts.

The bra that Oliver snapped that day, and for many days after, was a Dici. In the 1970s, all teenagers wore Dici, lured no doubt by the siren song of its famous television commercial: "Pretty as a bird up high, let me be free or let me fly, Dici—*Dici!*—or nothing..." In the commercial, an animated bra transforms miraculously into a seagull, and I could not have been the only thirteen-year-old disappointed when this never occurred in real life.

The soft-cup bras, introduced by Wonderbra in 1974 as an alternative to the conical breast jails of earlier decades, were meant to invoke the freedom of women's liberation. My mother brought them home from Eaton's in shades of sort-of white and dirty putty, and I wore them until they were sheer and sagged with use. At a certain point I escaped the nest, and soaring into adulthood like the Dici seagull-bra, became responsible for my own expenses. Because I was a woman, these would be great indeed.

How does every woman not become a Marxist revolutionary when she realizes the ridiculous price attached to her gender? Earlier this year I spent $500 on six bras, and not one of them is made from unicorn foreskin. Between them, they contain about as much material as a hand towel. Not one of them is the kind of majestic bra you'd find at Rigby and Peller, the London boutique that supplies underpinnings to the Queen, which I entered once and left almost immediately, so intimidated was I by the hushed and reverent atmosphere. I was an apostate in the temple of lingerie.

Women's intimate apparel is a $32-billion global industry, according to *The Lingerie Journal* ("Lingerie News from Top to Bottom!"). There is no equivalent outlay for men's underpants, which, as we know, are bought in bulk by wives and mothers on their lunch breaks. There is no Victoria's Secret television special in which men parade down a runway in their dingy Y-fronts.

In the thirty-five years I've been my buying my own bras, I estimate that I've spent about $12,000, and that includes the purchase of one particularly ill-advised demi-balconette printed with the Rolling Stones' lips logo (although it could be argued that having Mick Jagger's tongue on your boobs = priceless). That amount does not include "shapewear," camisoles, tights, slips, or any other garment aimed at keeping maverick female flesh under tight control (another $2,000). A single gut-shrinking panty girdle can run $100, a figure that would surely shock men—not that you would ever tell your man you'd bought one. That money could have instead purchased a trip to Greece, where I would have had an affair with a hot ferry captain, my breasts swinging gently in the Aegean breeze.

In the bottom of my purse are eight lipsticks: Stila, MAC, Revlon, Christian Dior. They have names like Vivienne and Runway and Rendez-Vous. Eight lipsticks when I have, at best, two lips. Together, they probably cost about $200. Some of them are rendered inutile because they've lost their lids and become tainted with shreds of tobacco, the tiny brown tentacles pressed into soft pink tips, like nerve cells seen under a microscope. The bottom of my purse is where my worst sins reside: vanity and sloth. I can no more resist a new lipstick than I can a social cigarette.

To be a human being is to be full of contradictions. To be a feminist woman is to walk around, daily, confronted with your empowerment and your dimin-ishment at the hands of others: The soap that tells you to live your best authentic self; the $200 vial of bee venom serum that tells you your authentic self is a wrinkly affront to the world at large. How often do we think about the astonishing amount of money we waste, as women, constructing a pleasing facade?

In 1990, Naomi Wolf coined the term "PBQ"— the Professional Beauty Qualification—to describe the punitive effects of accepted beauty standards on women. One of those effects was economic: We were selling ourselves short by buying into a crippling aesthetic model. As she writes in *The Beauty Myth*:

> The PBQ keeps women materially and psychologically poor. It drains money from the very women who would pose the greatest threat were they to learn the sense of entitlement bestowed by economic security: Through the PBQ, even richer women are kept away from the masculine experience of wealth. Its double standard actually makes such women poorer than their male peers, by cutting a greater swathe in the income of a female executive than that of a male, and that is part of its purpose... The few women who are earning as much as men are forced, through the PBQ, to pay *themselves* significantly less than their males peers take home.

I was twenty-five when I read *The Beauty Myth*, and it pierced my brain like a rocket. Empowerment feminism was at its height, and I justified the hundreds of dollars I spent on shoes as a professional expense necessary for climbing. If I were a mountaineer I'd buy crampons, wouldn't I? My feminism was rooted in the power of the ambitious self, but Wolf's doctoral thesis illuminated the oppression of the system, the structural traps that economics and history had laid for women. I wanted to give up the shoes and the lipstick and the expensive bras. I did not. What I could not yet comprehend was how much more I would spend as I grew older on the maintenance of my infrastructure. That I would become, in effect, the custodian of a picturesque but sagging bridge.

Twenty-seven years ago, Wolf pegged the cosmetics industry's value at US$20 billion (it is now US$460 billion, though this may not be a direct comparison) and the cosmetic surgery industry at US$330 million (it is now closer to US$20 billion globally, with nearly $14 billion spent in the U.S. alone). As the population ages, those figures will increase. You can have surgery to beautify your toes and your vulva, in order to compete with the foot models and porn stars out there. There is no need to visit Transylvania to obtain a vampire facial, a procedure that uses fresh blood cells to make you look less like a corpse.

Who am I to talk? My wallet lightens in proportion to vanity's rise. One week I decide to keep a record of this discretionary spending: I keep a separate pot of money for this, away from the family kitty. This seems retrograde and shameful, as if I am comic-strip Blondie hiding new hatboxes from Dagwood's judgmental raisin eyes. This is not even a particularly expensive week:

- $43: A lipstick I don't need. Up to nine. I now have enough tubes to form a hockey team.

- $47.50: Waxing. "Do you want me to do the patch on your chin?" the aesthetician asks. What am I supposed to say? No, please leave the goatee. I'm auditioning for Bearded Lady at the circus later. I nod, and she rips it away with one quick yank. The facial hair of middle age increases at a rate much greater than income. This must be what they mean by Freakonomics.

- $107: Advanced Retinol Night Treatment. It's a random collection of words that mean nothing to me, but I have read on a website that retinol dissolves fine lines. It's bullshit, of course. I am King Canute railing fruitlessly at the tide. The sea answers back: Relax, in the coffin no one will see your wrinkles.

- $113: Dermatologist's consultation fee: Because I live in the hellish No Man's Land where adult acne lives alongside wrinkles.

Between my eyes there are two deep grooves, as though a velociraptor has hooked me by its claws and dragged me screaming through the night sky. Yet I have refused the siren song of cosmetic surgery, at least so far. I don't want to abandon the face I'm meant to have. I worry that I'd look in the mirror for the years left to me and wonder, What was I supposed to look like? What was the face left on the cutting-room floor?

Around me, friends' faces change, their eyes become wider and their foreheads as smooth as peeled eggs, and sometimes they whisper, drunkenly, about what they've done and I try not to judge (even though I do, in my darkest heart). Mostly I wonder, How do you afford that? We are all cash-strapped; the money must have come from somewhere.

Until I realize that, for many of my friends, it's an investment: "Nobody at my office knows I'm push-ing fifty," one says. "They're all thirty years old. I can't afford to let them know." Several friends are unemployed and looking for work; it is competitive out there at the best of times. For middle-aged women, more so. What if that smooth forehead is the advantage they need? Not that anyone would hire on the basis of physical beauty, rather than a bursting resumé, right? How shallow would we have to be, as a people? How fucked would the world have to be?

I am afraid to tot up the cost of my vanity, because it is inevitably a cost to someone else: A trip I could have taken with mother, a thousand extra dollars in my children's university fund, money I could have given to charity. One day I find an article from the *Wall Street Journal* outlining four women's annual beauty expenditures, and suddenly I feel like a feral child raised by wolves. I am in the beauty wilderness compared with these women, three of whom spend US$20,000, some of it on things I didn't even know existed: What are hair vitamins, and would I be happier if I used them?

Hair vitamins, hair extensions, hair removers; breast enhancers, breast reducers; butt lifters, butt flatteners. It is extraordinarily lucrative to sell women the myth of bodily improvement. Last year, *Glamour* magazine made a short film illustrating this imbalance. In it, a mythical twenty-six-year-old Alison and Jason are presented in split screen. They wake up, shower, begin their beauty routines — curl enhancer for her, beard balm for him — as the cost of their respective public faces is totted up beside them. In the end, it is revealed that it costs Alison $1,832.55 to be a reasonably presentable modern woman, and $691.52 for Jason to be a man.

Glamour gets it. *Jezebel* gets it, too. The feminist website recently itemized "how much it costs to own a vagina," and came up with the figure $2,663.02. That includes birth control, tampons, UTI remedies, PMS relief, and preventative medical interventions like Pap smears. In Canada, where health care is publicly funded, that figure would be somewhat lower. Still, it's more expensive to own a vagina than a penis. Not to mention that the penis earns you more money in the end. But that's another chapter.

As Wolf notes in the updated foreword to *The Beauty Myth*, much has changed since the book was published: The pressure to remain youthful and thin is as bad as ever, or worse. On the other hand, young women of the fourth and fifth feminist wave are savvy and critical of advertising and social media in ways that only add to their power. They are often the producers of their own media: "On balance, I think we have come a long way. It is a great thing for young women and men today to grow up taking for granted that they are entitled to analyze and criticize the mass media ideals that are presented to them, and to define beauty, glamour and style for themselves."

Women may be free to criticize and analyze, but they're also still expected to pay more, as the prevalence of the so-called "pink tax" shows (this is the discrepancy in pricing for similar products marketed to men and women). In 2015, New York's Department of Consumer Affairs conducted a survey of hundreds of items, from jeans to razors to compression socks, in a study called *From Cradle to Cane: The Cost of Being a Female Consumer*. The report concluded, "Women are paying thousands of dollars more over the course of their lives to purchase similar products as men." The discrimination begins with children's scooters, and it ends with adult diapers; an entire lifetime, in other words, to be hosed.

Thank God for the young women at *Glamour* and *Jezebel*, for the researchers who uncover pink tax discrepancies, and for all the young women who question our unthinking acceptance of a system that rips us off at every opportunity. They are the ones in the past few years who've written hilarious Amazon reviews on products such as Bic's Crystal for Her, a set of pastel ballpoint pens with a slender barrel especially designed for a delicate lady's hand. As one reviewer noted: "I'd really like to buy a pack of these pens; but I probably need my father's or my husband's permission first."

They are also the activists — like the ones at Canadian Menstruators — who lobbied and fought to have the tax removed from sanitary products, which had been classified as "luxury" goods in Canada (how I survived my entire life without a Birkin tampon, I'll never know). These are the young women at the vanguard of the no-product movement, who refuse to waste their money on useless gunk in pots. These are the women who woke up earlier than we did. With luck, they will be the generation that grows up happy in its own skin, wrinkly though it may be.

NEVER ENOUGH: WOMEN, POLITICS, AND THE UPHILL BATTLE

IT IS THE day after International Women's Day, and I'm moderating a panel on the barriers facing women in political life. In these situations—barriers, politics, lawyers—I find that it's best to start with a joke.

"I hope you all had a chance to put your feet up and maybe have a glass of wine," I tell the lawyers of the Women's Law Association of Ontario, "because overthrowing the patriarchy is thirsty work."

They laugh. I am relieved. Any time you can get a laugh out of a bunch of lawyers in the bracket between 5 p.m. and wine o'clock is a solid win. It's also a good thing because I'm about to tell them something pretty shocking.

What I'm about to share is some polling data, released to coincide with International Women's Day, that reveals 54 percent of respondents think there are "enough" women in politics in Canada, and 4 percent think there are too many. Too many! I tell the audience: "A study this week from Abacus Data revealed that nearly 60 percent of Canadians think there are the right number of women in politics, or that there are already too many."

There is an intake of breath, and I see the women in the audience shaking their heads. Sitting next to me on the panel are Kristyn Wong-Tam, a Toronto city councillor; Farheen Khan, a community organizer who ran unsuccessfully in the last federal election; and Tamara Small, an associate professor of political science at the University of Guelph. They're all listening intently. None of them seems very shocked. They've all seen the sausage of democracy being made from the inside, and it is not picturesque.

Still, the right number of women in politics? As I say to the audience, did the people in that poll realize that only 26 percent of MPs in this country are women? Only 18 percent are mayors? Only three provincial premiers—and two of those have been in the news for the gendered abuse that's been hurled at them? Saying there are enough women in Canadian politics is like saying there are enough Nobel Prize winners in the National Hockey League.

The women on this panel know all too well the barriers that stand between them and elected office: a nomination process that leans toward incumbents, who are usually male; a first-past-the-post political system, also known as "winner take all," which discourages the selection of non-traditional candidates; a system that does not promote or financially support women, particularly those from racialized or LGBTQ communities.

On top of that, since the rise of social media there has been a particularly vicious, sexist public response to women in politics. More women are desperately needed in politics; research shows that women in elected office are better able to work across party lines and are particularly effective in policy-making. But given all the grief and hassle that women face in the political arena, you have to wonder, Why? Why do they put themselves through it?

I turn to the panellists, because I want to know what brought them into the arena. The answer, for both Wong-Tam and Khan, is the desire for change. Issues of social justice were close to their hearts (this jibes with research that shows that the desire to create change rather than personal ambition is the primary force motivating women to enter politics).

For Wong-Tam, the first out lesbian elected to city council in Canada's largest city, one of the main issues was gender equity, and as soon as she was elected she began working to establish an office for gender equality (she's also a driving force behind Women Win Toronto, which recruits diverse candidates to run at the municipal level). Khan, a long-time community activist who had seen anti-Muslim rhetoric at work in Canadian politics, wanted to be a fresh presence among the familiar faces in Ottawa — specifically, "a Muslim woman in a hijab."

When Wong-Tam decided to run for office, her parents were opposed: They were worried that it would be a brutal experience, and bruising for her. Khan, too, had to overcome the reservations of her family. Entering politics is hard enough for white, straight, middle-class women: those existing at the intersections can find the barriers insurmountable. For Wong-Tam, campaigning to win a riding that had been held by Kyle Rae, also a gay politician, sexuality wasn't a deal breaker for voters in downtown Toronto, but "there were other issues of discrimination and bigotry."

For Khan, the campaign was even more heated. Anti-Muslim sentiment was a feature of the 2015 federal election campaign, with the Conservative Party, at one point, floating the idea of a "barbaric cultural

practices" hotline. Barbaric practices, in this case, did
not mean playing Nickelback loudly or serving warm
beer. Everyone in Canada knew what it meant. It was
an anti-Muslim whistle sounded at precisely the frequency some voters wanted to hear.

Khan was advised to establish herself as "Canadian
enough" — emphasizing that she was born in
Mississauga and that her sister had served in the military. Although she received warm greetings at most of
the ten thousand doors she knocked on, there were still
troubling incidents. A man at a public meeting asked if
she'd impose sharia law if elected. One day, Khan stood
near her headquarters adjusting a lawn sign. A police
officer stopped and said, "Ma'am, what business do you
have in this neighbourhood?"

When Khan says this, a small gasp runs through
the room, and I see women in the audience shake their
heads. I'm also shocked, but shouldn't be: I know this
is what happens to Brown and Black men and women;
I know this theoretically, but not as part of my muscle
memory, not as part of a humiliating ritual.

Only a couple of weeks before, the Pakistani-
Canadian MP Iqra Khalid had introduced a motion in
the House of Commons condemning Islamophobia
and other religious discrimination; an anodyne, non-
legislative bit of political bread-breaking, you'd think,

on which all parties could agree. Instead, the motion became the subject of heated debate in the House, and venomous attacks outside. Protesters warned, against all evidence, that the motion would lead to something called "sharia creep," as if we were living in a horror movie and religious extremism was oozing up the steps from every decent Canadian basement.

Khalid was subject to a horrid amount of abuse, in emails and online: She was called a "terrorist" and a "draper head." She was told to go back home. She was threatened with harm: "Kill her and be done with it," said one message. The police stepped up patrols around Khalid's constituency office and her home.

Tamara Small, the professor of political science sitting to my left, isn't surprised about any of this. One of her fields of study is the swampy place where women and politics and online culture meet: "The discourse around women in politics is that women are still outsiders. Politics is a man's world, and all of these people are interloping. The Internet, more broadly, is not a particularly welcoming place for women."

That is not a surprise to the women on the panel, or those in the audience. I tell them that one of my colleagues at the *Globe and Mail* has recently been reaching out to men who abuse female politicians on Twitter, asking them, in a deadpan fashion, why they felt the need to call the Premier of Ontario a "cunt."

I'm relating this anecdote to the crowd, and suddenly I get to the word and freeze. Cunt. I can't say cunt in front of the Women's Law Association of Ontario! What if my grandmother in heaven hears? Instead, I say "the c-word," like a debutante, like I'm Jacqueline Kennedy at a tea party.

Then the absurdity of it strikes me: Trolls use the word cunt because they think we'll shrink from it. They think it's water on a witch.

"Cunt," I say, quite clearly.

And no one melts, or screams, or even blinks an eye.

WOMEN WON THE right to hold elected federal office in this country in 1921, three years after most of them had won the right to vote. (Shamefully, women of Asian descent were excluded, and Indigenous women were not granted the right to vote until 1960, alongside Indigenous men.)

Right from the beginning, the fun began. "Don't you wish you were a man?" an opposition MP yelled at Agnes Macphail, the first female member of parliament.

"Don't you?" she hollered back. Agnes, a progressive farmers' advocate from Grey County, Ontario, didn't have much time for nonsense. She wouldn't, as the lone female MP sitting in the House of Commons from 1921 until 1935, when the number of women in federal politics doubled to two.

Politics has always been a bare-knuckles game, even here in Canada, where the myth of politeness lies as thin as April ice on a pond.

"You damned pup," the sodden father of the country, John A. Macdonald, yelled at Oliver Mowat during a sitting of the House, "I'll slap your chops."

Fisticuffs, what fun. That's been the nature of male taunting: You're an idiot, a weakling, a traitor. The nature of insults aimed at female politicians is entirely different. It is gendered in two specific ways: First, it suggests an unnatural incursion—the woman has broken into a realm where she doesn't belong and isn't welcome. I like to think of this as the "back to the kitchen, wench" school of political theory.

Second, it is sexual or physical in nature. Female politicians are "bitches," "witches," "cunts," "whores." They are ugly and old and unattractive, or they deserve to be raped for punishment. Because they've voted for a carbon tax or for an anti-racism bill or an unpopular budget, they are inviting threats to be assaulted or killed.

The nature of the messages might not have changed much—and we'll skip gently over how depressing that is—but the language and delivery systems have. Consider that Ellen Fairclough, the country's first female cabinet minister (in the Conservative government of John Diefenbaker) was chagrined but not entirely surprised at the bitter comments directed her way in the late 1950s: "I'd meet people on the street who'd say, 'Why don't you go home and look after your house?'" she said, in an anecdote recounted in *Dancing Backwards: A Social History of Canadian Women in Politics* by Sharon Carstairs and Tim Higgins. "Well, I didn't make any obscene gestures, but I felt like it."

Sixty years later, Alberta MLA Sandra Jansen took the floor of the provincial legislature to read some messages she'd recently received: "Sandra should stay in the kitchen, where she belongs." That was one of the milder ones. She was also, in the measured consideration of her critics, a "bimbo," "a useless tit," and a "traitorous bitch." Jansen had made the mistake of crossing the floor of the provincial legislature to join the NDP government of Premier Rachel Notley, having abandoned a bid for the leadership of the provincial Progressive Conservative Party. She'd been forced out by rancorous attacks during the leadership race; the reaction to her floor-crossing proved her point.

Notley was no stranger to this kind of abuse. A progressive, NDP premier in Alberta was already as rare as a white tiger; add the fact that she was a woman and the tiger had a bull's-eye painted on its side. After she introduced a controversial carbon-tax measure, a crowd of Conservative Albertans chanted "Lock her up!" (Proving once and for all that we Canadians are destined to suffer cheap American knock-offs till the end of time.) More troubling, an investigation by the *Edmonton Journal* revealed that Premier Notley had been subject to more death threats than both preceding (male) premiers combined.

For a country so geographically vast and sparsely populated, Canada has at least managed to spread the misogynistic manure far and wide. One morning I listened to a report on CBC Radio's *The Current* in which an MLA from Manitoba and the finance minister from Newfoundland recounted their experiences. Nahanni Fontaine, an Objibwe member of the Manitoba NDP, talked about how she'd been called a "cunt" and a "whore" for speaking out about women's reproductive rights. Cathy Bennett, the Newfoundland finance minister, had been body-shamed online and threatened with death and sexual assault.

"It's a conscious attempt to silence and regulate what women can say and what women can do as female politicians," Fontaine said. Social media platforms needed to do a better job policing abuse. Canadians needed to do a better job standing up to this kind of bullying. Male politicians needed to be vocal allies. The host interrupted. Were male allies actually stepping up? Fontaine hesitated for a second.

"Perhaps not as much as I'd like," she said.

THERE ARE ANY number of barriers to women's participation in politics around the world, resting on countless cultural, social, and historical inequalities. But, if we're looking for a pithy explanation, I like this one from Phumzile Mlambo-Ngcuka, executive director of UN Women: "Men tend to choose those who are made in their own image."

More than one hundred countries have gender quotas as part of their political systems, some voluntary, some constitutional. Even then, female politicians account for fewer than a quarter of parliamentary positions worldwide: The number in 2016 was 23.3 percent, up from 22.6 percent a year earlier, and 13.1 percent in 2000. The Inter-Parliamentary Union, which compiles the figures, estimates that at this rate it will take fifty years to reach gender parity.

Canada ranks 62 out of 190 countries. Rwanda, which has gender quotas, ranks first, with women making up nearly 62 percent of the lower house of parliament.

You might be surprised that Canada doesn't rank higher, given that the current prime minister, Justin Trudeau, is often presented as a Feminist Dudley Do-Right in the international press. Indeed, there is something refreshing about a leader who happily calls himself a feminist. But there is talking the talk, and then there's actually walking to the bank, withdrawing cash, and using it to solve the problem.

When Trudeau announced that he would have an equal number of women and men in his first cabinet, the world sighed. He was asked why it had been so important to him to appoint so many women, and he shrugged with his father's insouciance and said: "Because it's 2015." You could almost see the little pink hearts dancing around his head.

Unfortunately, more than a year later, it's evident that it's not all rainbows and ice cream in Canada's feminist utopia. For one thing, Trudeau abandoned his promise of electoral reform: Canada's first-past-the-post, winner-take-all electoral system is generally considered unfavourable to women and other candidates from non-traditional political backgrounds. ("First past the post" means that the person with the most votes in a particular contest wins the seat, even if it's not a majority of votes; in competing systems, political representation is awarded according to the percentage of votes a party receives.) The Liberals promised the election of 2015 would be the last contested under the old rules.

After he'd been in power for a year, Trudeau's government abandoned the promise. Worse, he put a rookie female MP, Maryam Monsef, in charge of electoral reform — it was the political equivalent of asking her to stand in the sun holding a dead fish. Its failure became hers. Don't think other female politicians didn't notice. As Oxfam Canada noted in its 2017 Scorecard, "The Liberal government's bold feminist rhetoric has not yet translated into tangible policy and spending decisions that can really push the needle forward on gender equality."

A winner-takes-all political system is only one reason that women are blocked from power. They are also denied access to networking and fundraising opportunities that are available to men. They suffer from an incumbency handicap — those already in power are much more likely to maintain their seats. They are more likely to be nominated for ridings where a party's chances are already weak — the so-called "sacrificial lamb" theory identified by Melanee Thomas at the University of Calgary.

And, equally important, there are the barriers from within. Women are still less likely to put themselves forward for nomination; they may rebuff the first few attempts when they are approached. They cite as a major concern the loss of privacy that a life in politics entails. In 2015, the Women in Parliaments Global Forum produced a wide-ranging report called "The Female Political Career," which revealed some of the common anxieties women experience: "While both men and women express concern about the many pitfalls of political campaigning, women are more worried overall, particularly about gender discrimination, the difficulty of fundraising, negative advertising, the loss of privacy, and not being taken seriously."

They're right to be worried. It's a rough old world. As Julia Gillard, the first (and so far only) female prime minister of Australia, noted in a memorial speech for her murdered friend, British MP Jo Cox, gender hatred is simply a fact of life for women in politics. As a woman who'd been compared to a barren cow and been criticized for her physical appearance, she knew these issues intimately.

"Understand that you will encounter sexism and misogyny, and prepare yourself to face it and ultimately to eradicate it," she said.

She noted that women in public life could expect daily threats of violence; rarely but horribly, as in the case of Jo Cox's murder at the hands of a right-wing extremist on June 16, 2016, the violence online manifests itself in the real world.

Nor is there anything fresh in the misogyny: Gillard noted that the same insults that had been hurled at Hillary Clinton were also hurled at her. The U.S. presidential campaign was already a toxic river, the current gathering strength, when Gillard gave her speech: It showed "that this sort of gender discrimination isn't set to leave us any time soon."

A few months later, just before the U.S. election, comedian Samantha Bee sat down with some female heads of state to ponder the mystery of male hatred of female power. Norway's prime minister Erna Solberg talked about foreign diplomats assuming someone else in her entourage was the head of state, and Croatia's Kolinda Grabar-Kitarović pointed out that her face had been Photoshopped onto an actress from a porn film.

At the time of Bee's report, many still thought Hillary Clinton was likely to win: It's instructive now to watch the report and see the animosity of right-wing TV hosts, who called Clinton smug and shrill, and likened her voice to a cat being dragged across a floor. Their fear is a skunk smell; it should have been obvious to all of us. Or maybe we'd just grown so used to that smell that it was just *eau de* business as usual.

In Ontario, the province where I live, the animosity toward Premier Kathleen Wynne, a gay grandmother, is astonishing. Her government fell into various murky pits on the issues of fundraising and electricity pricing, but the response to those political scandals was distinctly gendered, in her case. The sophisticated critiques of her government policy included such online gems as "wrinkly bitch," "subhuman, dirty dyke," and "lying, cheating cunt."

At a press conference in early 2017, a reporter asked Wynne about these comments. First she paid lip service to voters' right to freedom of expression, as all politicians do, but then, her voice rising, she made a connection between the abuse and the province's future, a connection evident to any young woman with two eyes, a brain, and an Internet connection: "It discourages people from entering politics. And if I'm a woman—why would I do that? Why would I expose myself to those kinds of personal attacks?"

WHY, INDEED? Why, ladies, why? I'm actually pro-politician. I have trouble understanding the animosity and disdain we direct toward a group of people in whom we entrust many of the decisions that will shape our future. Why is wanting to be a politician a debased

ambition, but going to business school is applauded
by your gran and everyone in your high-school class?
It makes no sense. Yet we continue to deride anyone
who wants to seek public office. It takes a tough skin to
admit you actually want to be a politician—and that
hide better be made of titanium if you have lady parts.

One day in March, I venture to Queen's Park, the
seat of political power in Ontario, to find some answers
to the puzzle. I'm here to meet with a group of young
women who are potentially interested in a life in politics, if they don't choose something more reputable,
like used-car salesman or serial killer.

These young women are part of a group called
Daughters of the Vote, a nation-wide initiative of Equal
Voice Canada, which works to increase women's participation in politics. In a dark, wood-panelled room that
resembles an old-time gentleman's club, I talk to these
women about what brought them here, against all odds.

Azra is dark-haired and intent, and she's studying
political science at university: "When I meet strangers
and I tell them I'm studying political science, they say,
'Oh, politics?'" Her voice fills with sarcasm: "'That must
be *so much fun.*'" She sighs and shakes her head. "There's
such a taboo, especially around women in politics."

The other young women around the table listen
to her intently. They've all heard the same thing.

Maymuna is chill and confident. The daughter of
Somali immigrants, she's studying health policy at a
university in Toronto. "I've always had a passion for politics and social justice," she says. "I thought this would
be a good opportunity to network and get my foot in
the door and learn more about what it is I want to do."

For most of them, the political process is a mystery:
This day is the first step to unlocking it. "No one ever
tells you how to get into politics," says Samantha, a
teacher from Garden River First Nation near Sault
Ste. Marie. "Today I heard you have to volunteer, and
I was like, is that what we're supposed to do? There's
no path or someone to help you through it. That's a
major barrier."

If she does get into politics, Samantha says, it will
be at a local level, perhaps on her band council. Micro-
issues are her thing, the grassroots-level annoyances
that plague her community: Transportation. Access to
groceries. The other women all have pet issues they'd
like to advance — gender-based distribution of public funds, immigration, paid menstrual leave. They
are whole-heartedly aware of the systems of oppression they operate in, in a way that older feminists are,
perhaps, somewhat deaf to. When Maymuna says "Anti-
Blackness is a plague that's everywhere," the other
women nod respectfully and listen to her analysis of

the role that race plays in keeping women in her community from power. They are listeners. This, more than anything, may be the key to the future.

The future is a long way away: Equal Voice estimates it will take ninety years for the House of Commons to reach parity. Fully one-quarter of Canadians believe it will never happen. We will all be bitter dust then.

I'm not about to tell these young women that. They are already on trains bound for the horizon. Carly is planning to run for office as a school board trustee. She already works at Queen's Park, as an assistant to a member of provincial parliament. She's got a wealth of useful knowledge at her fingertips, such as the fact that women need to be asked to run for office an average of three times before they agree.

"It goes back to how we're socialized," she says. "We're not taught that this is a career we might be good at."

Across the table, Maymuna nods. She says that, right from the earliest days, she was taught to restrict her ambitions: "There's no opportunity within the school itself, and without the opportunities there's no way to build confidence. From day one you're taught to lower your standards for yourself. You're not taught to aim high."

They talk among themselves, nodding and listening. These young women are not the products of private schools or privilege. Two of them grew up below the poverty line. If they end up at Queen's Park one day, it won't be because they thought they belonged here, but in spite of the fact they suspected they didn't.

On International Women's Day, they will travel to Ottawa, and along with other Daughters of the Vote from every federal riding in the country, take the seat of their member of parliament (the young women are all between the ages of eighteen and twenty-three). For one symbolic moment, there will be a woman in each of the 338 seats in the House of Commons. Perhaps that's exactly the right number. I'm reminded of Ruth Bader Ginsburg's comment about when she thought there would be enough women on the United States Supreme Court: "When there are nine."

How many is too many? No one ever bothered to ask: How few is too few? At least not until very recently. The British historian Mary Beard is someone who has made morally compelling arguments about women in political power. We deserve to be equally represented in the decision-making process, not to raise so-called "women's issues" — which are really human issues — but because excluding half of the population is a waste of resources and acts against society's best interests.

"It is flagrantly unjust to keep women out, by whatever unconscious means we do so; and we simply can't afford to do without women's expertise, whether it is in technology, the economy, or social care," Beard wrote in the *London Review of Books.* "If that means fewer men get into the legislature, as it must do (social change always has its losers as well as its winners), I'm happy to look those men in the eye."

It is after lunch. The Daughters of the Vote have gathered to listen to three members of the provincial legislature — Conservative Lisa MacLeod, Liberal Indira Naidoo-Harris, and the NDP's Catherine Fife — talk about the challenges they'll face if they end up in elected office. There are the hours (brutal), the comments from social media trolls (even more brutal), the campaigns (so brutal), and the relentless attention to physical appearance (brutal *and* passive-aggressive).

"Why didn't you put on some lipstick?" Lisa MacLeod remembers one constituent writing to her. "You looked terrible on TV."

What happens if some of these Daughters of the Vote do make it into the legislature? For one thing, the hours will be more friendly: MacLeod arrived at Queen's Park to find that the house sat until midnight when it was in session. Those are hours that suit barflies, not babies. MacLeod realized that "if we wanted this place to be more open not just to women but to young women, we had to make it more family-friendly." Now the house rises at 6 p.m.

Each of these successful politicians is proof that it can work. They sold party memberships, fought for their nominations, found funding for their campaigns. Little by little, a different way of doing politics will emerge.

"We bring to the table a great deal of compassion and generosity, and an ability to work really hard," says Naidoo-Harris. "And we're very good at working with each other. We have the ability to be far more collegial."

In other words, without too much unseemly boasting, they are changing the system from within. Creating opportunity where there was none before. Changing the face of things.

"My daughter called me a 'difference-maker,'" Fife says, "and I thought, *I can retire now.*"

The young women in the audience smile and whisper to each other. All of them can relate to being teenage daughters, parcelling out reluctant praise to their mothers. Maybe some of them can see themselves here, one day, winning that praise from their own children.

The panels and discussion groups end. At the end of the afternoon, I say goodbye to the MPPS and prime ministers of tomorrow. I walk down a set of wide carpeted stairs, running my hand along the polished wooden bannister. The walls of Queen's Park are hung with portraits of men who once ruled this place, all of them remarkably similar in hair colour (grey), skin colour (pink), and chromosomal composition.

I haven't walked these stairs since 1989, when I was an editor with Hansard, the service that records all discussion in parliament and legislatures. I was fresh out of university. I rarely transcribed a female voice: There were twenty-one female MPPs in the legislature then, and all three party leaders were men. Now there are thirty-seven MPPs, and two of the party leaders are women—one of them is premier, the first in the province's history.

That is progress, I tell myself, as the old grey men stare off into the painted distance. That is so much progress.

IF THE WORLD WERE MADE OF LEGO:
A LETTER TO MY SON

Dear Griff,

I tried, I really did. When you arrived, I wrapped you in a white blanket, though I knew it was a bad idea to place a leaky infant inside a cocoon of snowy fabric. Blue was not your colour. You wore red and black and pink onesies. Mostly, you wore hand-me-downs.

When you were a toddler, I walked past the aisles of shirts that said "Tuff Stuff" and "Here Comes Trouble," pajamas covered with astronauts and dump trucks, clothing that told you, at two, how you should be in the world — who you should be in the world. At Halloween, I dressed you as neutrally as I could, as a pumpkin, a dinosaur, a bear. When you were old enough to choose your own costume, you went trick-or-treating dressed as a bag of Skittles.

You were always your own person. For a while, I tried to steer you down the path of righteousness by buying you the kind of wooden, handmade toys approved by co-op daycares. You were indifferent. I bought you watercolours and a tiny doll called Polly Pocket whose clothes fastened with magnets. You enjoyed the magnets. I tried to interest you in imaginary play with stuffed animals, but mostly you regarded them with suspicion. There was one exception: Your grandmother, who had a facility for buying the most terrifying toys, presented you with a stuffed vinyl cob of corn with a serial killer's smile on its little face. You played with that for a while.

I tried, in other words, to guide you between the peaks marked Boy and Girl. Perhaps it was a trivial exercise, but to me it was important. When the ultrasound told me that you were going to be a boy, I turned to the obstetrician in her plush Los Angeles office and yelped, "But I don't know anything about boys!" She gave me a look that said, *Apparently you know enough about them to get pregnant.*

I thought you might like the toys I had liked, Lite-Brite and Operation, or Barbie, whose hair I used to hack off with a knife and whose tiny nose I'd pierced with a safety pin. At the age of three, though, you found your one true love, which you would cling to with the single-minded devotion of a life-mating swan: the tiny interconnected blocks whose Danish name translates to "play well." You became a Lego man.

In truth, you became a Lego obsessive. You slept with your Lego catalogues under your pillow and carried them to school every day, their covers taped and re-taped. Your room became filled with hundreds of Lego mini figures — vampires, wizards, construction workers, Indiana Jones with his tiny whip — and your shelves crammed with the elaborate sets you got for birthdays and Christmas. If you ever needed to be bribed, we knew which bribe would always work. We had a loyalty card at the Lego store. We almost had to take out a second mortgage. Lego is not an inexpensive hobby. Many days I wished you'd stuck with the stuffed cob of corn.

Your awkwardness, the difficulties you had at school, they all vanished when you sat in front of a new Lego set. Some of them were astonishingly complex, their instruction manuals the size of a phone book. And yet, patiently and with remarkable concentration, you rapidly built each one: Hogwarts and Batman's cave and the pièce de résistance, which nearly bankrupted us, the Death Star, complete with a garbage room to crush mini figures Luke and Leia and Han.

Even now, as a handsome and wise teenager, the Death Star sits on your bookshelf. I think you still find it comforting, the way it all snaps together so perfectly, the way it can always be repaired. It adheres to the plan set out in its instruction manual; it follows a pattern; it makes sense. I think you like it for those reasons.

Here's the part I wish you didn't have to discover: The world isn't nearly as neat or comforting. You're already discovering it. I know, because I talk to you about what you read on reddit and 4chan, what you see on YouTube. You understand that it is chaotic out there, not just for girls, but for boys, too. There is longing and confusion, and the fact is that you're all alone in your bedrooms, electronically connected by this longing and confusion. In my day, at least teenagers had the mall.

I'm not sure that it's ever been as easy for boys as I imagined. The great American feminist bell hooks put it best when she said that patriarchy has no gender. She says about boys: "Patriarchy will not heal them. If that were so they would all be well." (I'm giving you her book *Feminism Is for Everybody* for Christmas, by the way. Please act surprised.)

Boys have been just as crushed and exploited by institutional sexism as girls have. Ask a boy who grew up gay or transgender in the 1940s or 50s; ask an old man if he felt, as a child, that he was encouraged to be a nurse or a kindergarten teacher. Ask him if he felt he could have stayed home to look after the kids. Boys have been suffocated by expectations, too.

The forces that built the patriarchy are reluctant to abandon the fort. They're clinging to the vestiges of poisonous masculinity as a weapon, even as that weapon threatens to destroy everyone. Boys are still told not to cry. They are told to "man up" as a way of avoiding their very real fears. Crucially, they are given no useful ways to deal with the anger and frustration created by a chaotic world.

And now the world seems particularly in pieces, and we are in a state of flux. Boys and young men are flung around by forces beyond their control. Women are still the victims of systemic discrimination, but we are making great strides, and men are still not entirely sure how to respond to a landscape that shifts before their eyes. The manual that their grandfathers were given is in tatters. Some men adapt; some respond with rage. I don't need to tell you that; you spend enough time online to know.

We used to keep your Lego manuals and catalogues in a desk, do you remember? They filled several drawers. Occasionally it would occur to me to throw them out, but then I'd think, *What if a piece falls off Ninjago: Temple of the Ultimate Weapon?* I mean, we had to sell your sister to buy that set. (I'm kidding! We only had to sell the cat.) Anyway, we would have been in a pickle if I'd thrown those manuals out. You would have been filled with frustration and anxiety, not knowing where the pieces went. You always liked to know the path ahead.

And I can't give you that anymore; the instruction manuals are gone. It fills me with more worry than I can say. The world seems more Jenga than Lego these days—teetering, haphazard, prone to collapse. Maybe all mothers through history have felt this way about the future, but it does seem a particularly confusing road ahead and the maps all written in vanishing ink.

You're lucky, Griff. You are like your dad: observant, even-keeled, intent on understanding how things work. You're lucky to have your dad, as a presence and role model. Look to him and you'll see how to be a good man. Look to your grandfather and your uncles and cousins. They all have something to teach about compassion and strength.

But in the end, you'll have to create your own manual for this life. I know you'd like to be able to flip ahead to the last page, to see a safe and solid and airtight construction, something that will last and not fail, but that's not the way things work. I trust you, though. I trust you to be able to build something worthwhile and true, even on shaky ground.

Your loving Mum

UNBALANCED

ONE EVENING, I find myself at a parents' council meeting at my children's school. It's a particularly hairy time at work and I don't really have the hours to spare, but I am experiencing a rare phase of can-doism, so I give in to the impulse. I really should volunteer more at school, I think, in the same way I think I should take up some form of exercise before my limbs atrophy and I'm reduced to one large ambulatory texting thumb.

We sit in a library that smells of cheese sandwiches, and I am the outlander. All the other parents are very kind, but they know each other already and are united in common purpose. The treasurer stands up to deliver his report. He clears his throat with some embarrassment. The number-one item on his agenda has to do with a deadbeat parent who's written an NSF cheque for the school's chocolate-bar fundraiser. The cheque bounced, incurring a $10 fee from the bank. Now the question is whether the council goes after this scofflaw to reclaim the original amount plus the bank's fee.

There is a horrified murmuring among the parents: They say *bounced cheque* in the same tones they might have once whispered *gonorrhea*. Bounced cheque! On a school fundraising drive! I am sitting there, half-listening, eyes on the snow falling in the darkness outside, when suddenly a blade of horror cuts through my reverie. I think of the notice I got from my bank. I think of the chocolates that have not arrived home with my daughter. The equation is stark: I am the deadbeat parent.

Slowly, I put up my hand. They turn to me, and suddenly they are the hostile farm folk in *Children of the Corn*.

"It was me," I manage to say. The treasurer looks at me blankly. "It was me," I repeat. "The cheque. It was my fault. It was an old chequebook—a defunct account—I should have thrown it out—"

No one says anything. They are mortified on my behalf. I am also mortified, but indignant. "I'm sorry," I say. "It's my fault. But I've been so busy..." It is the wrong this to say. It's like telling a roomful of alcoholics that the beer looked so good. They are all busy.

They did not write cheques on defunct accounts.

I slink out of the meeting and return, the next day, with a fresh payment for the charity chocolates — including the $10 bank charge. I am too embarrassed to ever show my face at parents' council again.

What would I say to them, if I had returned? That I was sorry? That I had tried, for years, to operate with a wire-walker's single-minded sense of purpose, but I was more Lucy Ricardo than graceful acrobat? That I had made the mistake of looking down and became unbalanced, and was falling? Why should I expect sympathy? They were all on the wire, too, with a baby on one hip and a shopping list in the other. The flailing was universal.

That evening of humiliation was the beginning of a realization, though: Maybe, to paraphrase Hamlet, the flailing is all. Maybe the flailing is life in full.

FOR THOUSANDS OF years, balance has been considered an ideal to pursue — but so, too, were other ideals, such as moral rectitude and piety. Those fallen away, we are left with balance as the shimmering modern grail, always just slightly out of reach. The irony is that the harder we struggle for it, the shakier the wire beneath us becomes, and the farther away the ground seems.

Now, of course, the discussion has been hijacked to mean "work–life balance" because the media conversation is dominated by people like me, who are in the scary middle of life, where there are many mirrors reflecting back our reality and none of them is flattering. All our metaphors involve frantic motion: juggling, running, flying, drowning. "I'm run off my pins!" I shriek down the phone at a well-meaning friend who asks how I am. We find weird comfort in our useless, circular motions, perhaps fearing that, like log-rolling lumberjacks, if we actually stop we'll drown.

The phrase "work–life balance" has been in use for nearly three decades. In 1991, the Wharton School of Business founded the Work/Life Integration Project, and ever since has been issuing sober reports about the need for more caring, flexible, intuitive workplaces. And yet the wire keeps jiggling: Blame the stormy economy. Blame the gorgeous distractions of technology. Don't look down.

You would need another lifetime to read all the books about work–life balance, never mind the studies, never mind the research. The quest for it is now yet another thing to be anxious about. Go ahead and read "Work–Life Conflict in Canada in the New Millennium" (2003) and feel your heart palpitate in anxiety and recognition. The authors of the study surveyed nearly 32,000 Canadians who worked in medium and large companies, and found 60 percent of them were experiencing high levels of "role overload"—having too much to do and not enough time to do it. I did not take to my fainting couch in surprise to learn that female respondents were more likely than men to report an excess of stress brought on by role overload.

Once, the equilibrium we sought was meant to be internal. The ancient Greeks wanted everything to be in perfect harmony—your wet and dry ingredients, your vapours and fluids, your bravery and restraint.

"Nothing in excess," said the Oracle at Delphi.

"The best and safest thing is to keep a balance in your life, acknowledge the great powers around us and in us," said Euripides, or at least we think he did, in one of the fragments that has survived (no one bothered to Tumblr their thoughts in those days).

The Greeks gave us the idea of the bodily humours in sync (eucrasia) and out of joint (dyskrasia). There were four humours, and in each personality a balance existed, depending on which particular juices were dominant: You could be melancholic (black bile), choleric (yellow bile), sanguine (blood), or phlegmatic (I think you can guess the fluid). Illness and emotional turmoil were the result of an imbalance in humours.

It's tempting to see the mania for self-quantification —the lifeblogging and the Fitbits and the wristwatch heart monitor—as the modern equivalent of the Greeks' search for equilibrium. Run five more kilometres and eat ten fewer grams of carbs and you, too, can achieve a golden state of harmony. At least until the next cookie beckons.

For the Greeks and the Elizabethans, balance was an internal mechanism affected by external factors: age, season, temperature. But for us, the concept is flipped on its head: Balance is not so much about what's inside as what's outside. It becomes about juggling competing demands on your time, and competing interests. It is about trying to keep twenty plates in the air, in the dark, with a small person clutching your leg.

In our swim-class-versus-project-deadline solipsism, we forget about all the other people seeking equilibrium: the grieving, the ill, the lonely, the poor, the terminally exhausted. I use "we" recklessly here, because what I'm really talking about are women who have the privilege of creating frenzy through the stacking of play dates and networking engagements and yoga classes: We can afford chaos. The really harried women are the ones who juggle several jobs, work split shifts, and do not have the cushion of private health insurance to break their fall. These are the women who are too busy to complain about being busy.

Years ago in London I interviewed Nicola Horlick, a high-profile fund manager and mother of five who was the obsession of London media: She wore heels and had a brood of children and managed assets and still the top of her head hadn't popped off! When I suggested to her that she deserved a cape and a red *S* on her chest, she shot me down, politely but witheringly: "The fact of the matter is that I would regard a woman living in a council estate who's a single mother because the man in her life has decided to leave her with three children, who has to work to support the children, who has no child maintenance, who lives in a tower block on the top floor with no lift—that's a superwoman."

Of course, she was right. And it's not just that we can afford chaos, but that chaos enriches our status. We are warriors of turmoil, and each added activity in a day, no matter how meaningless, provides an affirmation: The midnight lights in my kitchen illuminate tomorrow's bake-sale Nanaimo bars, just as they do in my neighbour's and all the houses on our street. Look at our industry. Feel the damp armpits of our accomplishment.

At some point, this juggling act has become a competition: I can keep thirty plates in the air. No, forty! As Brigid Schulte writes in her superb book *Overwhelmed: Work, Love and Play When No One Has the Time*: "Busyness is now the social norm that people feel they must conform to . . . or risk being outcasts." Schulte's book came out around the same time I was bouncing a cheque for the school fundraising drive; moving my family from one house to another; frantically rewriting the last bits of my first novel; raising two children; teaching a university course; working full-time as a journalist; shouting at my poor husband; and doing it all badly — except for the shouting part, at which I excelled.

Her book arrived like a gift from the goddess: Here, finally, was someone — a fellow journalist! — who felt as if she were doing too much, most of it haphazardly, and ruining her children along the way. Except that Schulte decided to do something about it: She would try "to get a handle on the contours of the crazy jangle of modern life, a state of being so intense that I had come to think of it as the Overwhelm."

Schulte's search for a solution to the Overwhelm took her to fancy restaurants in Paris (where she felt underdressed) and dads' groups in America and conferences around the world. And she came to a conclusion that I had started to come to, as well: Busyness is an addiction. Frenzy is a crutch we use to prop up our frail egos.

During her research, she visited Ann Burnett, a professor of communications and director of the Women and Gender Studies program at North Dakota State University, who studies round-robin Christmas letters for clues to how we transmit this particular anxiety-status to our loved ones. The letters, increasingly, are full of words like "hectic," "frantic," "whirlwind," and "consumed." It's boasting disguised as lament.

"My God," the professor told Schulte, after showing her the Christmas letters, "people are competing about being busy. It's about showing status. That if you're busy, you're important. You're leading a full and worthy life. There's a 'busier than thou' attitude, that if you're not as busy as the Joneses, you'd better get cracking."

I finished reading Schulte's book and reached out to friends about their search for balance (most had abandoned the search, and were instead drinking brandy from the rescue dog's collar). One of them, a single mother of two energetic boys, put it this way: "That exact moment when I feel I am juggling too many plates I ask myself, 'Why am I doing this? Who am I doing this for? Am I trying to be perceived as "busy" so that people will approve of me? Am I trying to prove my self-worth? Am I insecure about the way I am raising my children? Am I trying to please someone?'"

Another wise woman said: "Is there some magical

still spot that I can settle into in the eye of the storm? I think so, but I can't seem to stay in it very long. I find it at yoga and during morning walks . . . and then I lose it at work and end up looking for it in the fridge all night. I figure I ain't never gonna find it, so I might as well chill about being out of whack most of the time."

Chill out about being out of whack. Her words echoed in my ears as I sat down to dinner one night with my husband and children. We try to do this several times a week. The kids invariably want to sit in front of the TV watching *The Simpsons*, and sometimes we cave. Mostly we do not, and it's for my sake more than theirs, because I find it calming to cook, bizarre though it seems, and even more calming to sit with them and stare into the eyes of the people I love, brown eyes and brown eyes and blue eyes. Even when those eyes are rolling at me in exasperation.

On that night, I was trying to do ten other things, all of them badly. I had two speeches to write. There were 6,587 unread emails in my inbox, and Microsoft was threatening to cut my electronic umbilical cord. Unlike the people in Schulte's book, I didn't feel smug. I just felt slightly nauseated, because there was a mysterious message written on my hand and I had no idea what it said.

I am constantly writing notes on my hand because all the remembering-places in my head are full. My

husband invariably shakes his head when he sees my
sullied hand and reminds me of the Google family cal-
endar he has lovingly set up on my computer. I wished
I'd listened to him: The combination of my terrible
handwriting and indelible ink combined to foil my best
intentions. There was an important message scrawled
on my body, in Sharpie, but I couldn't read it. This was
doubly tormenting: My body would forever be branded
with my lack-wittedness.

At dinner, I showed my hand to my family. "Can
any of you read what this says?"

"Wow," said my husband. "If only you had a magical
electronic device that could record these things for you."

"Does it say 'hi-bye'?" my son asked.

"Why would I write 'hi-bye' on my hand?" I said,
perhaps a bit too shrilly.

My daughter grabbed my hand, pondered it for a
minute. "I think it says 'worry.'"

I snatched my hand back and stared at it. Maybe I'd
become the kind of madwoman who writes "worry"
on her hand, just in case she forgets, for five minutes,
to worry. Then the absurdity of the situation hit me,
and I burst out laughing.

"You know what I'm going to do?" I said. "I'm going
to cut off my hand. Then I won't have to think about
it anymore."

"I have a knife," my daughter said.

The next day, with the ink still mockingly black on my hand, I realized that the scrawled message was actually the set of initials of someone I'd forgotten to email. One more plate hit the floor, but it didn't matter. I'd become used to walking around ankle-deep in crockery. We all had. If I may paraphrase T. E. Lawrence, or at least Peter O'Toole playing T. E. Lawrence: Certainly, it's a mess. The trick is not *minding* that it's a mess.

One morning I find an old journal. I was always terrible at keeping journals. I felt the same way about them as I did love affairs and cigarettes: I was only ever interested in the first, freshest stretch. This one documents a desert between its green suede covers. In early 2000 I had left Toronto with my husband to live in Los Angeles, where he had a job and I did not. I knew no one, though the geography of the city was intimately printed on my brain; I'd been crazy about old movies since I was a child, an obsessive in black and white.

The street on which we settled, in a decrepit building mockingly named the Saint-Tropez, was a bridge across time. Vinyl-clad sex workers, unfailingly cheery, anchored one end; at the other sat the yellow stucco bungalows of Charlie Chaplin's old studio. The city was full of everything, and my life was empty. I had no work visa, and so no work. I dreamed about having a baby and waited, month after month, for it to happen.

Lassitude is a prophecy that fulfills itself. The less I worked, the less I wanted to work. A trip to the drug store could take a whole day: the planning, the preparation, the actual excursion, the recovery. The frenetic movement of my life in Toronto — I'd been the executive editor of a women's magazine — had slowed to a standstill, like a rocking horse come to rest. The air quivered with my self-pity.

On the day of my thirty-fourth birthday, I taped into my journal a poem I'd been carrying around between the pages of a book. It was called "Table," by Turkish poet Edip Cansever, and I would read it in the morning, when the day stretched unfilled ahead, and at night, with the desert behind. It suggested a future in which I wasn't alone in an apartment building populated largely by porn stars and valets waiting for their hip-hop careers to begin. I longed for the day when I wasn't unburdened but, like the table, sagged with abundance:

<u>Table</u>
A man filled with the gladness of living
Put his keys on the table
Put flowers in a copper bowl there.
He put his eggs and milk on the table.

He put there the light that came in through the
    window.
Sound of a bicycle, sound of a spinning wheel.
The softness of bread and weather he put there.
On the table the man put
Things that happened in his mind.
What he wanted to do in life.
He put that there.
Those he loved, those he didn't love.
The man put them on the table too.
Three times three make nine:
The man put nine on the table.
He was next to the window next to the sky;
He reached out and placed on the table
    endlessness;
So many days he'd wanted to drink a beer!
He put on the table the pouring of that beer.
He placed there his sleep and his wakefulness;
His hunger and his fullness he placed there.
Now that's what I call a table!
It didn't complain at all about the load.
It wobbled once or twice, then stood firm.
The man kept piling things on.

When we left Los Angeles and moved back to
Toronto, my table groaned. My baby son I put there,

and my father who was so difficult, and the house with the cracked walls. My ambition. The job that put me in charge of nearly thirty people, and woke me at 4 a.m. every morning to a dull hum of dread, I put those on the table. I climbed on the table to make sure everything was safe, and though it felt like the whole thing was going to collapse, it wobbled, then stood firm.

What if balance is overrated? The British philosopher and psychoanalyst Adam Phillips makes an elegant case in his essay "On Balance": "Faced with the stresses and strains of everyday life it is easy now for people to feel that they are failing; and what they are failing at, one way or another, is managing the ordinary excesses that we are all bested by: too much frustration, too much bad feeling, too little love, too little success, and so on."

But what if we accepted a simple proposition? That we are, as Phillips says, "too much for ourselves." We are overstuffed with longing and frustration and ambivalence, but these are home-base emotions, and we should not flee from them. It's in the chaos that we find ourselves.

In fact, we are most alive when we are off-balance: We speak of being "swept off our feet" by love or "bowled over with happiness" when a child graduates. We lose balance when we're captivated by a person, or a thought, or the sight of something beautiful or disturb-ing. We are over the moon, and has there ever been a less stable place? But that is where we find the greatest joy, with the ground rushing up to meet us, falling or flying, or both at the same time.

THE STORY OF MY MOTHER

"AND THEN," my mother says, holding up one red-lacquered nail, "you had to hold your finger in the dial and wait until precisely 9 a.m. to dial the last number." She is remembering one of her main duties as a nurse in a major Toronto teaching hospital in the 1970s: making golf appointments for one of the surgeons in her department.

"He'd be very upset if you didn't get exactly the tee time he wanted," she says. "So you had to be quick on the trigger." She is eighty-five years old, her face turned to the sun, and she is cradling her favourite drink, Pinot Grigio-and-whatever-juice-was-in-the-jug. I've heard this story a hundred times, and it still makes my blood boil. My mother shrugs. Golf-dialling was among the lesser humiliations she and her fellow nurses suffered. They were groped, and underpaid, and made to stand when the doctors came to the nurses' station. They were required, periodically, to shave the chief surgeon's back.

My mother is made of stories, like Scheherazade, like Borges's library. She is made of stories the way a margarita is made of tequila. She is made of stories that are part 1950s horror comic book, part *Black Narcissus*, and part *Carry On Nurse*. Her best stories have a mad, surreal quality—the product of working in a deeply Catholic hospital run by nuns at a time when the world was twirling in its disco shoes and snorting poppers outside.

When I was a child she would come home and present these stories over dinner. One female patient had inserted a lemon in a particularly private place, and the exhausted resident who was confronted with the task of extraction said: "If I'd known there was going to be a party, I would have brought the gin." There was the man who complained of pain in his abdomen until a blue crayon was extracted from his bladder. There was an overly amorous pet monkey attached by his jaws to a woman's bottom.

In those years, there were no public places to celebrate sexual fetishes, which were still labelled deviancy.

If things went wrong with your particular jam, you went to emergency and relied on the kind doctors and nurses to sort it out for you. And if the doctors and nurses went home and chuckled about it to their families, perhaps it was a small price to pay.

Years later I would come to understand this humiliation in a particularly acute way. It's probably better to just say it quickly and get it out there: When I was in my twenties, I accidentally swallowed my friend's engagement ring and ended up in the emergency room where my mother had worked. The very same hospital! You could hear God laughing even with the doors closed. Many years later I heard that my X-ray was still posted in the doctors' lounge, the emerald ring clearly visible on its journey toward my sphincter, and freedom.

My mother's stories drew a picture of a world that was dark and strange and thrillingly absurd. She was the kind of nurse patients loved and remembered, and sent notes to after they'd left hospital. "That poor man," she'd say, as she launched into a story about a patient who'd had the wrong eye operated on, "such a terrible thing." Her compassion refilled itself day after day, and it was tempered with a streak of pragmatism. If she noticed someone was a smoker, she'd lock the door to the room, crack the window, and they'd light up together, leaning on the sill and puffing up to the sky.

My friends love her for her stories. I'm fairly certain they only tolerate me as a conduit to Mildred. Gay men love her, but so do children and the mentally troubled. She adores parties, and when I invite her to one, I will often find her at centre of a rapt huddle, the odd word or phrase drifting out: rupture, lawsuit, *and then I saw a little curl of smoke above his testicle and I knew something was wrong.*

As I grew older, I realized that what had seemed hilarious was in fact horrifying, and the stories she told had at their roots a diminution of her professional worth. As a student nurse, she had to kneel if the hospital's priest walked by carrying the sacraments of Holy Communion; one afternoon he walked past and my mother obediently dropped while her fellow student, carrying two full bedpans, struggled to her knees.

The nurses across Ontario formed a union, finally, to ask for what should have been given to them long before. They went on strike for better pay, and my siblings and I stayed up late painting slogans on cardboard. The next day she and her colleagues picketed the hospital, and a man driving by rolled down his window to bellow, "Florence Nightingale would turn in her grave to see you!"

She has long since retired. "Ah, well," she says, as we sit in the sun on my porch. "It's easier for you girls these days." Like a cat, she loves a patch of sun. There is no bitterness in her words: I think she is truly happy that things are easier for me. I look over at her, the blonde hair she will never surrender and the vibrant red lips she applies many times each day, and I marvel once again at her strength. She has overcome things I can't imagine: a gothically horrible marriage to my father, separation from him and the drug addiction that followed; depression, poverty, illness, and the death of my brother.

All of her stories begin this way: *Have I ever told you.* Often, she has already told me. On a surprising number of occasions, she has not. I have known her for five decades, and she still surprises me. As we sit on the porch, she throws me a curveball. "Have I ever told you about the time I was supposed to go to Tasmania?"

I turn to look at her. I'm usually starting to drowse when I hear *Have I told you,* but this is new.

"No, you haven't."

"It was after I graduated. My friend Ruth and I were going to go to Tasmania. She had family there."

"Tasmania — are you serious? Did you have jobs lined up?"

My mother shakes her head. "It just seemed like a great adventure."

Now I'm sitting up on the porch sofa. She has all my attention. "But you didn't go. Why not?"

She turns to look at me, and I'm pretty sure I already know the answer. "Because I met your father."

WHEN I MOVED with my family to London in 2004, Mildred pretty much moved with us. That is, she visited for three months at a time, twice a year. It was an adventure for her, and she is a sponge for adventure. I got free child care, companionship, and an in-house storyteller who was equal parts Monty Python and H. P. Lovecraft.

"Have I ever told you," I heard her say, as I descended the stairs one morning, "what human brains look like?" She was sitting at the breakfast table with my six-year-old son, who was enthralled. "Most people think they're pink. But really they're grey. They look like a bag of grey sausages."

We were alone a lot, the two of us, in the company of two young children and the crates of wine that came to the door every week. My husband was on the road, reporting from whatever country was on fire: Iran, Libya, Greece. *My Daddy never takes me to Poland!* our son shrieked one morning, and it was hard to argue with that.

"Did I tell you," my mother said over the evening meal, "that we almost didn't have butter for dinner tonight?" I was half-ignoring her, as I often did, as all adult children do with their parents. One day my children will ignore me.

"The only reason we have butter," she continued, "is because the Holy Spirit reminded me."

That got my attention. I am an atheist—the rotten apple fell far from the tree—but a story about the Holy Spirit at the grocery store will get me every time.

"Yes," my mother said, happy now that I was listening. "I had just left Waitrose, and I was just passing the pub, when I heard a voice in my ear say, 'Mildred, did you remember to get butter?' And you know, I hadn't." I did not ask her how she knew it was the Holy Spirit—perhaps there was a password. Later, when I repeated the story to my husband, he said it was the only good argument he'd ever heard for organized religion.

She was, like most Catholics, death-enthralled, the essential blitheness of her character tinted with a touch of the macabre. I inherited this trait from her. Cemeteries bound us. We both loved walking in them, reading the stories told by the tombstones. London is rich in gravesites: We visited Karl Marx and George Eliot in Highgate, Samuel Johnson and Charles Dickens in Westminster Abbey.

In St. Pancras churchyard, we found the marker where Mary Wollstonecraft once lay (the great feminist philosopher's grandson moved her remains to Bournemouth decades after her death). Wollstonecraft died of childbed fever, and her absence left a hole in her daughter Mary's heart that was never entirely filled. Her words would give Mary purpose, though: As a child, she was taught to read from the letters on her mother's headstone. Later, sixteen-year-old Mary would lie on her mother's grave with her lover Percy Shelley, and they would read Wollstonecraft's works of radical philosophy to each other.

I became slightly fixated on the story of Mary Wollstonecraft and Mary Shelley, two women who refused to be bound by convention, who used their stories to transcend their unhappy lives, whose histories are linked for all time thanks to the writing they left behind—particularly Shelley's novel *Frankenstein* and Wollstonecraft's *A Vindication of the Rights of Women*. They were separated in life but their words spoke to each other, stories of pain and loss that echoed across centuries. Mary Shelley was obsessed with the mother she lost, and would read and reread Wollstonecraft's seminal works; her mother's voice bled, across the years, into her own.

They were both abandoned by their fathers: Wollstonecraft by her alcoholic and profligate father Edward, and Shelley by hers, the political philosopher

William Godwin, who preached radicalism but was horrified when it appeared in his own house. After Mary ran away with Percy Shelley and bore his child out of wedlock, her father refused to have anything to do with her.

Mother and daughter suffered the social ostracism of a society that thought women's highest perch could only be obtained through lawful matrimony. Wollstonecraft also bore an illegitimate child, her first daughter, Fanny. They both poured the pain of exile and abandonment into their writing. The men they loved, fathers and husbands, disappointed them without cease. They would live, instead, in art.

This was nearly impossible for women at the time. Little changed in the period between Wollstonecraft's intellectual peak in the late eighteenth century and her daughter's a few decades later: "In the early nineteenth century, women artists were by definition monstrous," writes Charlotte Gordon in her magnificent biography of the mother and daughter, *Romantic Outlaws: The Extraordinary Lives of Mary Wollstonecraft & Mary Shelley*. Horace Walpole called Wollstonecraft "a hyena in petticoats."

Wollstonecraft published much of her early work anonymously, as her daughter did, twenty years later, with *Frankenstein*. When Shelley was revealed as the novel's author, Gordon writes, "The knowledge that a woman had written *Frankenstein* was so shocking in many circles that it hurt the book's sales." *Frankenstein* is often seen as Shelley's psychological payment to her mother, the creature destroying its creator. In all ways, her mother gave her the stories that defined her life.

My mother came with us to Rome over Christmas one year. We spent a day wandering in the Cimitero Acattolico, the Protestant cemetery where Percy Shelley's ashes were buried after he drowned in 1822 (in perhaps the most famous recorded case of white man's overconfidence, Shelley was an avid sailor who never learned to swim). We wandered among the tombstones in the late afternoon sun as the graveyard's resident cats slunk in and out of the shadows. We found Shelley's grave, with its famous epitaph taken from *The Tempest*:

> Nothing of him that doth fade
> But doth suffer a sea-change
> Into something rich and strange

My mother took my daughter by the hand, and they tried to coax the cats from their hiding places. I wandered by myself through the tombstones and the angels and urns. Most of the graves held people lost to history. I looked for women's lives. Each grave held a thousand untold stories, the heart of someone's family. Each terse epitaph was compressed with meaning, like the tiny medieval prayer boxes that contain an entire biblical scene carved within: "Her loss was as that of the key-stone of an arch," I read on one gravestone. And another: "She saw. She knew. She created beauty."

She saw. She knew. She told stories.

"HAVE I EVER told you," my mother says, "about the machete your father brought along on our honeymoon?"

We are in Tim Horton's having a coffee. I stare at her, because I'm pretty sure she didn't just say what I think she said.

She nods, delicately picking at her muffin. She is recovering from what the doctor in the emergency room called "the largest ulcer I have ever seen." To cheer her up, I've taken her to see a show of brightly coloured glass at the Royal Ontario Museum. We are both hot, peevish, and tired. These days she moves at a snail's pace, and as we crept through the museum, around the obstacles of giggling, oblivious students, my fists were clenched in frustration.

"A machete? Why did he bring a machete on his honeymoon?"

My mother shrugs. There was so much of my father that was unknowable, and since he's been dead for seven years, we'll never know. She had her revenge on him in the end, in her particularly passive-aggressive way.

"Your mother can't let me die in peace," my father liked to say. "I have to die bothered."

Sure enough, as he lay in his casket, she placed a rosary between his unbeliever's hands. It seemed presumptuous, considering that while they were technically still married, they'd been separated for thirty years. When I observed that he may not have wanted to carry a rosary through eternity, she shrugged and walked away. My mother shrugs the way Baryshnikov danced.

So. The machete. He placed it under the driver's seat as they set off for their honeymoon in Quebec. My paternal grandmother, my nonna, who was quite crazy and did not particularly like my non-Italian mother, had told her earlier in the day: "You be good to Nino. You can always get another husband, but I can never have another son." Late in the first night of their marriage, my father woke up screaming from a nightmare that he was trapped in a dark place. (We are a gothic family; subtlety is not our forte.)

It is the first time I've heard the honeymoon story. I suggest to my mother, perhaps cruelly, that she should have taken a hint and fled while she still could. Immediately, I feel ashamed. It's not something she hasn't thought of a thousand times herself.

My parents were married for fifty years. That is, they married in 1957, and when my father died fifty-two years later they had never divorced. However, they had not lived together for thirty years. Just before Christmas 1979, after many attempts and false starts, my mother finally got it together to leave my father. We were relieved, my brothers and my sister and I. In place of the screaming and the sound of Corningware dishes smashing the kitchen window, there was blessed silence.

My father deserves his own book, if not his own library. I could tell you that he was a tyrant who cast a shadow over my childhood, and also a bohemian who opened my mind's windows. He was eccentric, charismatic, and on occasion thoughtlessly cruel. There was something of Aleister Crowley about him: *Do what thou wilt shall be the whole of the Law.* He once gave my ten-year-old nephew, his grandson, a book of Victorian illustrated erotica as a present.

Some of his eccentricities I fashioned into stories for other people's delight: There was the time he called 911 from his hospital bed to complain that the nurses were torturing him. When we were children, we never went to the movies: We either went to plays and concerts (when there was money) or, when there was not (much more frequent), we were taken to witness natural disasters. Rivers flooded, trains derailed, buildings collapsed — these were all family expeditions.

My father had an illegal police scanner and would monitor it carefully. If he heard of a particularly ferocious fire, he would load us into the car, even in the middle of the night, and drive us as close as possible to the flames, inching past police blockades. It was thrilling, sometimes, and terrifying, mostly, to be his child.

He was also a terrible husband to my mother: angry, unfaithful, and petulant. I understand now the source of his pain: His own mother had suffered what would surely be diagnosed today as schizophrenia. She believed her family was trying to murder her, and was institutionalized. My father was forced to take her to the mental hospital in a taxi, with a police escort, while she leaned out the window screaming in Italian that her son was trying to kill her. He was fifteen years old. I came to have sympathy, much later, for the forces that bent him. Neither of my brothers were interested in the forces that bent him, and were largely estranged from him for years before his death.

My mother's stories rarely include my father, for obvious reasons. You might want to relive someone else's maelstrom, but not your own. Especially if it was a maelstrom that nearly destroyed you. My sister and brothers and I rarely talk about the dimmer corners of our childhood, because what lurks there seems too ludicrous to be believed, too baroque to have existed in 1970s Toronto. There was a rule in our house, for example, that if we ever caught my father hugging my mother, or showing her any physical affection, we were to come between them and break them up. For this service my father would give us 25 cents, a shiny quarter. It was a system so perverse, so clearly damaging to our young souls, that sometimes I wonder if I imagined it. But my imagination isn't that dark and borderless. I'm not William Faulkner.

And then my mother escaped. That's one ending of my mother's story, and when I think about it as a feminist parable, she is Jill Clayburgh riding public transit into a sun-drenched future, supporting her children and her mother in a high-rise tenement on a nurse's salary, growing as a woman and a human, travelling, reading, becoming the red-lipped, yellow-haired octogenarian who drew people to her at parties. But there was also another reading of her story, involving an addiction to pills and a stint in rehab, and depression, and a lot of offering pain up to God, which is a Catholic's way of avoiding therapy. You could look at her on either path, and still see that she was a hero.

DID MY MOTHER make me what I am? Do I tell stories because she did? Was I afraid to trust men, for so long, because of what one man did to her? Am I feminist because I saw the way the world treated her, and the way she refused to respond with cruelty in return?

She would never have thought she was living a feminist's life, even as she lived it. She supported her children, after my father kicked us out of the house when I was thirteen. (He told us to choose between them. We chose her. He made us leave that night, our possessions in green garbage bags.) She was a founding member of her union. She was a voracious reader, a seeker of knowledge, a collector of strays and outcasts.

I became entranced with the histories of other mothers and daughters who shared stories. My favourite books from childhood were Laura Ingalls Wilder's *Little House on the Prairie* novels. Years later, I would curl up on the bed with my own daughter, reading the books together, knowing the fraught history of Wilder and her daughter, Rose Wilder Lane. United by a libertarian ideology they wanted to camouflage as children's literature, riven by professional jealousy, mother and daughter collaborated through gritted teeth on some of the most famous juvenile literature of the twentieth century.

I did not tell my own daughter this: She was

enchanted by young Laura's corn-cob doll, by the pig's bladder made into a football. It seemed criminal to shatter her illusions. One day she could discover for herself that the authors of the *Little House* books probably loathed each other a good part of the time but soldiered on so that they could awaken the American people to the evils of big government. Then she could decide if she'd read those books to her own daughter. The Circle of Life.

As I was writing this book, the great writer and actress Carrie Fisher died. It was a blow to millions of people. It was a blow to me. I felt as if no one would ever make me laugh again, the way she had with her novels and memoirs. Other people loved her as Princess Leia, but for me she was always Carrie the Writer, inimitable, semi-depraved, dark as baked-on sin. Consider this passage from her memoir *Wishful Drinking*, also the title of her one-woman show. She is describing her father Eddie Fisher's adulterous affair with a grieving Elizabeth Taylor, which was a front-page scandal in the 1950s: "He first dried her eyes with his handkerchief, then he consoled her with flowers, and ultimately he consoled her with his penis."

Damn, I thought when I first read that line. *I will never be as good as Carrie.* It was a small consolation that none of us would.

Carrie Fisher died in a Los Angeles hospital, less than a week after she'd suffered a massive heart attack on a flight home from London. Two days later, her mother, Debbie Reynolds, died of a stroke. Had Debbie died of a broken heart? Was such a thing even possible? The heart knows when there is not enough glue in the universe to keep it together.

If any mother were to die of a broken heart, surely it would have been Debbie Reynolds. As adults, Debbie and Carrie lived in adjacent houses on the same property: the mother who'd been abandoned by a philanderer and a fraudster, and the daughter who'd been abandoned by a man for another man. Over the years, their relationship had been troubled, and at one point they were estranged. But they enjoyed each other too much to be apart for long. As presented in the documentary *Bright Lights*, they lived in raucous harmony, a kind of Grey Gardens for the age of sanitized voyeurs.

In her books, Carrie set her own struggles with drugs and mental illness, hilariously, against her mother's eccentric, show-must-go-on fortitude. Once, Reynolds suggested that her husband and her daughter should have a child together, because the resulting infant "would have nice eyes." On another occasion, Reynolds gave her daughter—and her mother—a vibrator for Christmas. I picture Carrie Fisher cackling with joy as she pulled the vibrator from her festive stocking, recognizing, as all writers do, priceless material when they see it.

"After I was finished thinking she was this trippy lunatic," Fisher writes in *Wishful Drinking*, "I realized that she was pretty fucking amazing...I've watched her for my whole life, and she's got this insanely strong life force. It pours through her veins and her muscles, and her heart. She's remarkable."

I've watched her for my whole life, and she's remarkable.

MY FATHER DIED in the summer of 2009. Afterward, our little Addams family gathered to sort out his things, his weird trinkets and weirder books, his boxes of mysterious files, the detritus of a long life. We were oddly giddy, my brothers and my sisters and me, as we sorted and remembered the infrequent peaks of joy that rose from the storm clouds. We were high on post-stress chemicals. Until, that is, I found the letter.

The letter sat in a dusty box with a collection of receipts and coupons and the bits of ephemera that constituted my father's life. It was addressed to my mother.

I recognized the writing on the envelope as my grandfather's hand—that is, it was a letter to my mother from her father, addressed to her at the hospital where she worked, not at our home. And it said, on the outside, "to be delivered personally or returned to sender." My grandfather hadn't wanted anyone but my mother to open it, and I would soon see why.

"Um," I said, holding the letter up for my brothers and sister to see. "This is weird. A letter to Mom from Gramps. I wonder why it's with Dad's stuff, if it's her letter."

"Why don't you read it," my brother said.

Feeling slightly dirty, but only slightly, I slid the letter from its faded envelope. I read its contents. Afterward, I sat in uncharacteristic silence.

"Well?" said my other brother. "What is it?"

This is what it was: A letter from my grandfather to his daughter, telling her that he loved her, and that he knew she was unhappy, and that she should think about leaving her marriage. He worried that she was being mistreated by my father. He worried about his grandchildren. He wanted her to know that she could come home, any time, that her parents loved her and would welcome her with happy hearts. If she had made a mistake, it could be fixed.

She probably never saw the letter. If she had, why would it still have been in my father's possession? It crushed my heart to think that she had never seen it, never known of her father's love, and worry, and offer of sanctuary. The weight of my mother's story is too much sometimes. It is a stone, a boulder, a mountain.

The next day, we brought my mother a few things from my father's house: some CDs, a couple of books, a vase. I sat on the sofa beside her and pulled the letter out of my purse.

"We found this, too."

My mother took it from me, and ran her fingers over the front. I watched her face for any hint that she recognized it.

"That's my father's handwriting," she said.

"I know," I said, and lied: "I haven't read it."

She stood up, taking the letter with her, and went into her bedroom. Taking with her the story I'd never heard anything about before. Maybe she'd just forgotten. Maybe it had been too painful for her to tell. A little while later, she came back without the letter, lipstick freshly applied, dry-eyed.

My curiosity could not be contained. "So? What was in the letter? What did Gramps have to say?"

"Nothing," my mother said. "It was nothing."

FOUR LIONS

OVER THE YEARS, I have been fortunate to interview an extraordinary range of people. I often think about them and their generosity. Especially at Thanksgiving. As my mother goes around the table asking everyone what we feel grateful for, and each one of us mutters "this family," with varying degrees of truthfulness, depending on how much we're fighting that day, I secretly think: *All of you who have shared your stories with me.*

All of you. Every person. Every Second World War codebreaker or bomber pilot, every single mother and survivor of domestic violence, every politician, opera singer, racehorse trainer, gardener, engineer, clown, and translator of Klingon (oh yes, folks, it's a job). I've interviewed presidents and prime ministers, poets and carpenters, a dominatrix who went to the same elementary school as me, the first Canadian woman in space, and the geneticist who revealed that the bones found in that car park really did belong to King Richard III (that geneticist, Turi King, is also a woman, by the way, and a Canadian).

Each of those interviews was a revelation, a magical window into the mind of another human being. There are times when this bounty makes me feel like Roy Batty at the end of *Blade Runner*—"I've seen things you people wouldn't believe"—except that I am neither murderous nor a cyborg. At least I'm pretty sure I'm not a cyborg.

Not all encounters were equal. I have come away disappointed from interviews with famous people who I was sure would blow my mind, and I have become deeply enchanted with people who were unsung but passionate about some particular aspect of the universe (birds, stars, trees, their own misbehaving children). I never knew, when I set off with tape recorder and notepad, which way a conversation would turn.

Sometimes, an interview would leave an indelible impression, a finger pressed into the soft loaf of my brain. I would walk away, dazed, and get on a train or bus home, staring out the window, my mind churning with thoughts and feelings. *I have to remember this,*

I would think and scribble pages of illegible notes to myself. And then I would write the story, and it would be published, and sometimes readers would notice and sometimes they would not, but the impressions remained, unchanged.

Those interview subjects lingered in my head, and I would hear their voices years later, what they said and how they said it. I've chosen to write mini-portraits of four women—three household names and one who should be—because each one of them impressed me in some profound way. I remember each of their voices vividly. Each one of them taught me something about the value of using your voice, for education or survival or self-expression or just to hear it lifted in rage.

"DO YOU KNOW HOW MUCH YOU FRIGHTEN PEOPLE?"

It was spring 2008, and my cab driver was lost. He drove in circles around the Essex countryside, past fruit trees in bloom and ancient silos where hops were once stored. His aimlessness seemed deliberate; he may have been trying to protect me.

"You're going to visit *her,* are you?" he said, eyeing me in the rear-view mirror. He did not want to say her name, in the manner of Puritans who felt that naming Satan's imps would summon them to the fireside. Eventually, he found the right address and we pulled up beside a beautiful old stone farmhouse. *She* was standing at the top of a set of stairs, staring balefully at the cabbie as he drove away.

"I think that one must be missing a synapse," she said, and her flat Australian drawl carried on the wind, perhaps as far as the taxi driver's ear. Not that she would have cared if he heard; she never cared, which was one of the reasons I was there.

I'd wanted to interview Germaine Greer for years. No, I hadn't. Yes, I had. Let's just say I'd wanted to interview her but had lived in mortal dread of being granted permission. What if she used my guts for tennis strings? What if she picked her teeth with my finger bones? On film, I had seen her pitted against Norman Mailer in *Town Bloody Hall*, the documentary about the notorious sexist pig showdown/debate in 1971 New York. In person, I saw her deliver a speech about Australian Aboriginal art, where she took apart a heckler with the brio of an Edwardian duke sitting down to a seven-course meal. I'd read her newspaper column, in which she eviscerated everyone from Princess Diana to Steve Irwin, the late crocodile hunter, whose death by stingray, Greer argued, was the poetic revenge of the animal world.

In short, I was afraid. The previous year, I'd sent a tentative message to her assistant, asking if Greer might be available for an interview, and received this reply: "I'm afraid under no circumstances does Professor Greer do print interviews." I slunk back into my cave, ashamed at my relief.

And yet, only months later, I stood in her yard, watching as she descended the stairs slowly — she'd recently broken her ankle. With her cane, she shooed away a peacock named George (for Byron) and called her dogs, Magpie and Michael. Dogs and birds she loved; she could not abide cats. "Disastrous animals. They eat their weight in small animals every day," she said, hobbling to sit by a bench in the shadow of her farmhouse. She fixed me with blue eyes, vivid behind spectacles. "I mean, what is a cat? The poor bugger's genes are so fucked up."

This struck me as odd, because if I were to imagine Greer as an animal, it would be a cat: solitary, independent, capable of taking down prey with one well-aimed swipe. Cats would not be the only target in our conversation, which was supposed to centre on her biography of Ann Hathaway, *Shakespeare's Wife*, but instead ranged from her disappointment with modern-day feminism to her disappointment with Hillary Clinton to her disappointment with Ian McKellen's cock (which she saw from a distance, when the celebrated actor was playing Lear and decided to display it for the audience. "Great, pale, rubbery thing it was," she said, shuddering. I asked, gingerly, if she didn't find it at all impressive. "In an elephant's trunk-y kind of way," she conceded.).

She stretched out in the sun—yes, like a cat, or some other predator that enjoys toying with prey foolish enough to stray into its path. And yet there was nothing particularly fierce about her, except her pronouncements and her disdain for many of the failings of the modern world, including, but not limited to, the politics of feminism, the town of Stratford, and Shakespearean actors. She was tall and beautiful in the manner of a wild-crested and free-roaming bird; cat and bird at once.

What I remember from that afternoon is the nature of her pronouncements, which were candid, unfettered, sometimes bonkers, and always entertaining. At sixty-nine, she seemed a liberated thing: I wrote that she had the quality of a medieval siege engine cut loose from its moorings, barrelling down a steep hill. It is a rare thing to meet a woman, especially a famous one, whose opinions are not wrapped in equivocations and apologies and packaged for mass consumption.

She had just written a column stating that Uluru, the giant rock sacred to Australian Aboriginals, should be closed to the public, because the public is debasing it. "People say, do you only write about things that get people mad? Do you go looking for trouble?" She flexed her bad ankle in front of her. "No, but when you're dealing with crass stupidity you have to call it. If they don't like it, tough."

Some of those opinions were so out of step with accepted thought that they got her in deep trouble — such as her (painfully wrong, in my opinion) argument that trans women aren't really women and that they cannot understand the oppression that women face. Years after our interview, there would be calls for her to be banned from giving a speech at a college campus over her views on transgender issues.

But I thought, as I sat talking to her in the warm June sun, that her appeal lay not in what she said, always, but in the way she said it — in the power and vigour of her outspokenness, in her lack of respect for orthodoxies. She steamed forward on a solo path, "the dreadnought women's libber," as William Buckley once called her. Living by herself in the English countryside, writing her books, accompanied by her animals and her quick, questing mind, she seemed free from the dinner-party straitjackets that the rest of us wore, the boring adherence to a set of principles on which our in-group could agree.

I had just finished rereading *The Female Eunuch*, the dizzying, discursive bestseller that made her name in 1970 and provided one of the incendiary rhetorical bombs of second-wave feminism: "Women have very little idea of how much men hate them." It's a loopy, non-linear book, and not one that can be read like an IKEA manual. It is not a guide for building a movement. It is a guide to blowing up an oppressive system, though.

I was not surprised that she became neither a leader nor a member of any movement. She was intellectually unsuited for a narrow path, and constitutionally unsuited for anything requiring teamwork and consensus.

"I can't do committees and meetings and agendas. I'm too undisciplined, too impatient," Greer said. "You wait and wait for people to get to the point. I can only utter my barbs and wait and see what happens. If I was involved in feminist politics I think I would be terribly, terribly, disheartened. Miserable."

We sat for a minute, watching the birds in the trees. She asked if I was hot in the sun. I was not. I would have been happy to sit for hours, listening to her. Later, I would think about whether there was a trade-off involved—the solitary house, the freedom it entailed—and wonder if it was too facile an observation. I wish

I'd asked her. Instead, I asked if we were living in a post-feminist world, and she snorted.

"As far as I'm concerned feminism has yet to begin. We haven't even worked out what the enemy is."

We spent a couple of hours talking about Shakespeare's poor, forgotten wife, and the general contempt that history shows for wives of famous men. She talked about the dons who refused to have women in their lectures when she was studying at Cambridge University in the 1960s (her doctoral thesis was on the subject of marriage in Shakespeare's comedies). Then the photographer arrived to take her picture and she looked down at herself, inordinately pleased, and said: "Tits look good!"

When I left—a different cab driver this time, one with all his synapses—I looked out the window and thought of something Greer had said. It would stay with me for years after, a kind of motto, though I was utterly incapable of living up to it. She'd been talking about her reputation, and where it led her. "When someone says to me 'Do you know how much you frighten people?' The only thing I can say is 'Not enough. Nowhere near enough.'"

"HUMAN INTELLIGENCE, HUMAN COURAGE, HUMAN PERSEVERANCE"

Downstairs in P. D. James's beautiful home in West London was a table where she spread out her materials—notepad, dictionary, thesaurus, pen—and wrote longhand, aiming for ten thousand words a month, a book a year. After the day's work was done on one of her immensely popular detective novels, she would take up another of her tasks—being matriarch of her family, or giving a lecture on judicial policy, or attending the House of Lords, where she sat as a Conservative peer, Baroness James of Holland Park.

Just thinking about it exhausted me. I wanted to be Germaine Greer but, on the other end of the decorum spectrum, I also wanted to be P. D. James. I had such a girl crush. Can you have a girl crush on a woman who's eighty-five?

Phyllis Dorothy James was that age when I first met her, and she had just published her nineteenth novel. It was called *The Lighthouse*, a mystery featuring her poetry-writing detective Adam Dalgliesh, whom readers adored but whom I found irritatingly mopey. I loved the books; I just wished Dalgliesh would occasionally punch a wall or spill sauce on his shirt.

By the time she ushered me into her exquisite sitting

room, with its pale green William Morris wallpaper, I was already in love. She'd written a terrific sort-of memoir called *Time to Be in Earnest*, a year's worth of diary entries—though she loathed the idea of diary-keeping—in which the past kept seeping in, cold and dark as floodwater. And what a past it was: her parents' unhappy marriage, her husband's suicide, her blazing late-in-life success as a novelist. All these things she did with an unshowy, uncomplaining commitment to the task at hand. She would be a mother. She would work. She would write.

Phyllis wore a lavender blouse, her thick grey hair swept majestically up. There was a heavy silver pendant around her neck, which swung forward as she poured tea from a china pot. All around her were the trappings of an intellectual life, quiet acknowledgements of accomplishment: early editions of Charles Dickens and Jane Austen, photos of her children and her grandchildren and great-grandchildren. In a small office, tucked away, was a picture of her wearing velvet-and-ermine ceremonial robes at the state opening of the House of Lords. Otherwise, there were no indications of her worldly success, no gaudy testaments to vanity. This, of course, made me love her more.

We chatted a bit about her new mystery novel, but what I really wanted was a glimpse into her creative heart. What had been the grit in her oyster? Now that she could buy all the pearls she wanted, what kept her going? Her memoir offered intriguing glimpses of pain, including her parents' miserable marriage. ("Of course it lasted," she wrote. "Marriages, however unhappy, did in those days.")

Her own marriage was loving but shattered by forces outside her control. Her husband, Connor Bantry White, had been a doctor in the Second World War. He returned home devastated and spent much of the rest of his life in mental hospitals, dying by suicide in 1964. (She wrote and spoke very little publicly of this, although once in a radio program she said simply, "I found him.") James and her two daughters moved in with her in-laws, and she would write at night, when she came home from her job in the health civil service. She'd write on the train when she went to visit her husband. She snatched moments when she could. This devotion to craft is something I, who rarely commits to a whole season of television, can barely fathom.

Or perhaps writing was solace? I suggested it cautiously, but she waved away this nonsense with a ringed hand. "Solace? No, I don't think so." A compulsion, then? "Yes, I think so. One psychiatrist said that creativity is the successful resolution of an internal conflict.

There's something in that. For people in any form of art, there is a compulsion."

Whatever it was, I found her devotion — to her day job, and her writing dream, and her family, and not least to public service — deeply moving. And she wasn't po-faced about it; she had a macabre streak, at odds with her pretty house. As a child, she would imagine which little classmate might die before the end of summer. Her mind was filled with poison and knives and hands that shoved bodies off high cliffs, but she placed those thoughts where they belonged, on paper, just so, and then poured the tea.

FOUR YEARS LATER, I returned to that beautiful house, and I must have been moaning about my early (and never-ending) midlife crisis, perhaps about the way that the flesh was sliding down my face like the icing off a badly baked cake.

Phyllis was having none of it. Briskly, she placed her hand next to mine on the gleaming wooden table. Hers was pale, veined, elegant, adorned with silver rings; mine needed a wash. "You can try to hold back time, but you can't do anything about your hands," she said. "Compare them, my dear. An old hand and a young one. There's nothing you can do about it."

My hands did not seem so young to me. Her old hands continued to make do and mend, in the words of the old wartime posters. She had finished her twentieth novel, a Dalgliesh mystery called *The Private Patient*, while recuperating in hospital from heart surgery. Now, a few days before her ninetieth birthday, she was working on a secret book she didn't want to talk about, lest it didn't work out.

It wasn't a mystery novel, at least not a typical one: She dreaded the idea of churning out novels, like Agatha Christie or Ngaio Marsh, merely because her publisher and her public clamoured for them. Yet she told me something that day about the appeal of writing mysteries that made me understand her inner cogs and gears a little better: "No matter how difficult problems are in life—in your own life or in the life of a country or society—in the end they can always be solved, not by divine intervention or good luck, but by human intelligence, human courage, human perseverance."

It's what she had done, wasn't it? Overcome the difficult puzzle of her own life through the application of human intelligence, human courage, human perseverance. I left Phyllis's house that day as I always did, determined to be less of a whiner. Less lazy. I would work harder on the novel I had just started. She made me want to be better. Not that I would have ever told her that; I could imagine the look of horror on her face.

WHEN I SAW her a final time, the following year, her secret book had been revealed: She'd been working on a novel called *Death Comes to Pemberley*, a sequel to *Pride and Prejudice* with a mystery at its centre (it became an enormous bestseller, like her other novels, and then a miniseries).

She was ninety-one, and there was a walking stick propped next to her while we talked; I couldn't remember it being there during our last visit. Not that she had slowed down in any noticeable way. After I left she was going to get dressed for a reception at 10 Downing Street, the prime minister's residence.

If anything, age had liberated her. Only at ninety-one did she feel ready to commit an act of lese-majesty and tread on the ground of her beloved Jane Austen. She had loved Austen for eight decades, ever since, at the age of ten, she'd had to choose between two books on the shelf at Sunday school: *Pride and Prejudice* or *Jessica's First Prayer*. You can guess which one she took home.

For years after, Austen was her great passion. She watched, bemused, as other novelists took Austen's characters and twisted them into outrageous shapes, sending them off to fight zombies or time-travel through history. It was not quite drawing a moustache on the *Mona Lisa*, but close.

"There are about seventy previous sequels to *Pride and Prejudice*. Some of them are quite extraordinary," Phyllis said. "Zombies and sexual goings-on, the most extraordinary things. I think she'd be pretty fed up about those!"

Why should an accomplished writer who adored Austen not be allowed to play with characters who were, as she put it, "so much the furniture of our minds?" And so she did, crafting an excellent mystery while also giving us a glimpse into Fitzwilliam Darcy's inner thoughts and his marriage to his beloved Lizzy.

Here was the final lesson that Phyllis taught me, about the freedom that arrives like a gift with age. Yes, I'd seen a hundred magazine cover lines screaming "The Best Years of Your Life!" and "Gain Years, Gain Confidence," but it had always seemed like so much magazine bullshit. And, as I say, I was in my forties and preoccupied with my melting face. But Phyllis, like Germaine Greer, was living proof of the fuck-you ticket that is issued along with your senior citizen's bus pass. Who cares what critics think? Who cares if Jane Austen would roll in her grave? The curtain would come down soon enough, all noise drowned out.

Death Comes to Pemberley was the last book that Phyllis would write. Three years later, I was sitting in my winter-dark living room in Toronto when I heard the news that she'd died. Immediately, I felt a choking sorrow. Something good and noble had moved out of the world, a stout heart, a craftsman. But it felt useless, just sitting and mourning. Idleness solved nothing. I went to my computer and began to write a column about Phyllis, about what it meant to lead a life well lived.

"SO NOW GET UP"

When Hilary Mantel was in law school in England, she started suffering terrible internal pains. No one took a young woman's agony particularly seriously, especially if it was situated uterus-adjacent. She went to visit a psychiatrist, who diagnosed the source of her anguish: It was stress, he said, caused by overambition. He wondered if law school was too taxing. Mightn't a dress shop be a better outlet for her talents?

What none of the doctors knew, but Mantel suspected because she was consulting surgical textbooks, was that she was suffering from a severe and undiagnosed case of endometriosis. The drugs prescribed for her psychological and physical misery led her to a mental-health clinic. There, she began to write a short story about a changeling—that is, about a woman in rural Wales whose baby is snatched and switched for another. When she outlined the story to her psychiatrist—the one who prophesied a dress-shop career—he said "I don't want you writing."

I don't want you writing! And you, Picasso, put down that stupid paintbrush. There are tomatoes to be packed. When I came across that anecdote in Mantel's wonderful, spiky memoir *Giving Up the Ghost*, I almost shrieked. What if she had given up writing? A tragedy for the world of literature. A tragedy for me, personally: She is my favourite living author.

I'm firmly of the opinion that a journalist should never meet her heroes. They will invariably disappoint, not because of their own failings, but because they have been constructed out of some bright-sky material in the journalist's brain and will necessarily be duller in real life. But, in a few cases, some of which I document in this chapter, they do not disappoint, but leave an indelible, electric impression instead. Such was the case when I took the train one day to meet the woman whose latest novels had made her, against all expectations, a smash success.

Hilary Mantel's little town on the Devon coast was ridiculously pretty, as pretty as a village from a BBC detective series in which the killer is the vicar or the lady who puts up the best pickles. It was prettier than it had a right to be. It actually had a café called the Cosy Teapot.

And here lived a woman with a singular gift for inhabiting dark and sinister worlds, past and present, and finding the humanity and humour in them. Most of her novels were contemporary, though it was the most recent pair, set in Tudor England, that had made her a star. They were all novels born of her body's pain, written in spite of that pain, or perhaps because of it — how better to transcend the body than imagining a world that is different, distant, peopled with intriguing strangers?

There was no darkness in the cheery flat overlooking the sea, or the woman who answered its door. Mantel had the round, bright blue eyes of a china doll, even though her smile suggested a doll possessed by a mischievous demon. The phone was ringing when I entered and hardly stopped (it was answered by her husband Gerald McEwan, a man she had divorced once and married twice). The phone rang because, after a life of critical acclaim but popular obscurity, she had achieved a whacking great success with her novels about the life of Thomas Cromwell, *Wolf Hall* and *Bring Up the Bodies* (a final novel in the trilogy, *The Mirror and the Light*, is in the works).

"Everything that has happened since the publication of *Wolf Hall* has astonished me," she said, leading me slowly over to an overstuffed sofa. "I should be shock-proof, but I'm not. It's not a world I thought I'd be in."

That world, for a woman sometimes confined by illness to an area close to her writing desk, was a huge and liberating one: two Booker Prizes for the first two novels of the trilogy, smash success stage and television adaptations, millions of copies sold. Even stranger, this popularity hadn't arrived on the wings of vampires or wizards or S&M–loving billionaires, but through highly literary, dense novels narrated in an archaic tense called the "historic present." The books are not for all readers, and some complain that they're too complex, too allusive. Yet, there they remain, the unicorn of the publishing world: thorny masterpieces that sell like iPhones.

"You can't go wrong with Henry VIII," Mantel said with her sly smile. We both knew that the real star of the books was Thomas Cromwell, the king's reserved and compelling *consigliere*, who began a pauper and ended with his head at the mercy of an incompetent executioner. The entire narrative arrived in one swoop, she said, when she heard a voice in her head say the words "So now get up." They are the first lines in the first novel; they will likely reappear at Cromwell's ignominious end.

We chatted about *Bring Up the Bodies*, because that's what my newspaper and her publisher wanted (in fact, I had had to sign a non-disclosure agreement, which is pretty hilarious for a novel outlining some of the best-known episodes in Western history). Really, I wanted to talk to her about her own narrative: about how writing saved her, about the children she never had, about the intersection between the two. In my mind, she was heroic, having overcome pain and rejection, and quietly plugged away writing extraordinary novels that hardly anyone noticed.

I wanted to ask her about pain, because I, too, had felt my guts hollowed out with knife-spasms. She had endometriosis; I had Crohn's disease. I wanted to ask how she had overcome that pain to write — not just overcome it, but fed it into her furnace, watched it burn and char, the blackened ash turning into words on the page. She began researching her first novel, *A Place of Greater Safety*, an invigorating, vast novel about the French Revolution, on "days [she] was half well." No publisher wanted it, at least not at first; it was the first novel she wrote, the fifth to be published.

But I didn't ask her about her pain, nor shared mine. It would have been too weird. This wasn't a therapy session. But I could ask her about the unborn children she wrote about so beautifully in *Giving Up the Ghost*;

they were the phantoms of the title, "stretching out their ghost fingers to grab the pen." Ambivalent about whether she wanted to have children, the decision was made for her when she had to have a hysterectomy at twenty-seven.

"You had that psychiatrist," I said, "the one who diagnosed you with an excess of ambition."

"Oh yes," she said, with a light laugh. The laugh of someone who is generous in triumph. "He recommended I go work in a dress shop."

Could she ever imagine a doctor saying such a thing to a young woman now? "Probably people wouldn't dare couch it in those terms, but things have really not got a lot easier for women," she said. "The agenda of control has just become less overt. People still have a tremendous struggle in trying to live a woman's life, and trying to bring up children and go out there and be an actor in a world that is still so much a man's world. We still work to a man's timetable and a man's agenda."

The obvious question to ask, as she watched me calmly with those huge blue eyes, was whether there would have been fewer books if there had been any children. Could one make such a crude and lumpen equation? Would she have been as productive, if she had to stumble over the famous pram in the hallway that Cyril Connolly said was the death knell for artistic ambitions?

She answered quickly, in her cool, bright voice. It was not the first time she'd thought about the question. "Probably not. Something would have suffered. To be honest, I'm quite a maternal person, and I'm a bit of a control freak, so it probably would have been the writing. Someone said one child equals two books."

Well, that was a relief. I now had an excuse for four books left unwritten. I did have one book at home, a comic novel that I'd dithered over for three years. I worried, at that point, that it would never be published. I worried that it would.

On the train ride home, and on many days since then, I thought about Mantel's immense productivity, her genius for creating character and situation, her unwillingness to be cut down by rejection or dismissal or fear. Years later, I would have a coffee mug on my desk. It says, in an antique, typewriter-y font, "Nevertheless, she persisted." I try to live up to it. And on some blessed days I do.

"THEIR DEATHS WOULD HAVE SIGNIFICANCE"

When I sat down with Setsuko Thurlow in her Toronto apartment in the summer of 2017, I wasn't sure how to tell her about the strange connection that joined us across decades and continents and world history. I wasn't even sure I wanted to tell her. My family's livelihood was connected, oddly and tangentially, to her family's destruction. How do you bring that up in polite conversation?

I had come to talk to her about the devastation of Hiroshima, which she had survived as a girl. But first, we would commune over a plate of midsummer cherries. "They're very good this year," Setsuko said, as she wheeled over to her fridge on her walking frame. She handed me the plate to carry into the living room, as I wondered whether to bring up our connection. It certainly didn't seem like the right moment.

I felt Japan everywhere: In Setsuko's accent, in the plate of cherries, in the beautiful silver wedding kimono hung on the wall. "Not mine," she said, pointing to the kimono. "I didn't wear that one." In fact, she married her Canadian husband Jim in a traditional North American bridal dress, in Washington, D.C., in 1955. They couldn't get married in Virginia, where Setsuko was studying at university; the state banned whites from marrying non-whites.

But all that came ten years after the day that changed her life — the day that changed the world, really. Setsuko is a *hibakusha*, one of the survivors of the atomic bombing of Hiroshima and Nagasaki. Now she is eighty-five, and tired, but also elated because her life's work as a disarmament activist — necessary work that had seemed painstaking and fruitless for so long — was finally showing some small reward.

She settled herself slowly onto her sofa. Her legs had been bothering her, the result of recent trips to the United Nations in New York, where she had given survivor's testimony in support of a treaty banning nuclear weapons. The ban passed, with 122 countries voting in support, and although it's largely a symbolic document, it's a monumental one in the eyes of *hibakusha* and other disarmament activists — a first step to outlawing the last remaining legal weapons of mass destruction.

Setsuko told her story at the United Nations, the story she's told countless times over the years, to audiences of children and adults, politicians and veterans. Her voice shook at the UN, and some of those listening wept.

Setsuko recounted it for me in her Toronto apartment, while I wondered if I should tell her my small piece of the puzzle. An elegant woman, she wore a fuchsia blouse and bold red lipstick, almost exactly the same shade my mother wears. They are only one year apart in age. When Setsuko spoke, her eyes were lost in the middle distance, and sometimes they welled with tears. But she made a decision, long ago, that whatever pain remembering brought, it was much preferable to the numbness of forgetting. She chose her voice over silence.

"I feel it's really important to tell my story," she said. "I made a vow to my loved ones, my schoolmates, to family and friends, that their deaths would have significance. It would not be in vain. I would not forget this. I would do my best till my last breath."

She clasped her hands in her lap, perched on the edge of her sofa, and remembered that day again.

On the morning of August 6, 1945, she was Setsuko Nakamura, sitting on the floor of her girls' school in Hiroshima, listening to an army official drone on about duty to the emperor. For the past few months, she and her grade 8 classmates had been used as cheap labour by the army, sewing buttons on uniforms and packing cigarette boxes. In recent weeks, they'd trained as decoding assistants in preparation for the final Allied invasion of Japan.

But the Allies didn't invade Hiroshima. At 8:15 a.m.,

Setsuko saw a blinding blue-white flash out the window and felt herself lifted through the air. She came back to consciousness in pitch darkness, and the only sound she heard was her classmates calling for their mothers, or for God. She was pinned under something. She heard a male voice — a soldier, perhaps — tell her to crawl toward a patch of light. He shoved her. She crawled. When she got free, she turned to look at the wooden schoolhouse, now engulfed in flames, her classmates inside.

She felt no panic. She felt nothing. She was thirteen years old. "All around, everything was destroyed," Setsuko said. "There were some moving objects, but they didn't look like human beings. They were moving about slowly, silently. That silence was a spooky thing, I remember. Nobody was screaming."

She joined this ghostly procession, shuffling along in a morning that was dark as night. The 20-kiloton uranium-based atomic weapon had detonated 2,000 feet above Hiroshima, causing unimaginable damage. Setsuko used her hands now to try to demonstrate: Skin hanging in shreds. Eyeballs hanging out. Intestines hanging out. Thousands were incinerated immediately, or died within the next few days. By the end of the year, 140,000 people would die as a result of the bomb in Hiroshima, 75,000 from the plutonium bomb that fell on Nagasaki three days later.

With two classmates, she came to a military training ground where thousands of victims lay dying. They
cried for water, but Setsuko and her friends had no way
to carry water. Instead, they took off their blouses
and soaked them in a nearby stream, and pressed
the dripping cloth to the mouths of the dying. That
night, Setsuko and her classmates sat on a hillside and
watched the city burn. She wondered if her house had
burned, her favourite dress with it.

Her parents found her in the morning. They had
survived the blast, but Setsuko's sister and her four-
year-old son had been in the city centre visiting the
doctor and were horribly burned. For the next several
days, Setsuko and her parents nursed them as best they
could, with no water, no food, and no medicine. Her
sister spent her last days apologizing for failing her son,
while the boy begged for water.

When they died, soldiers came and tossed their bodies into a pit. They poured in gasoline and lit a match,
turning the burning corpses with bamboo poles.
Setsuko watched, alongside her parents, and felt no
sorrow. Worse, she felt nothing. This numbness would
haunt her, a secondary casualty of war.

"For years after I thought, *What kind of human being
am I?* My dear people were being treated not even like
human beings, and I didn't even feel sadness."

She paused in the telling of her story. I had the urge to take her hand, which would not have been very professional. Instead, I told her a bit about my interest in nuclear disarmament — how I co-founded a nerdy group called Youth for Peace in high school, which attracted almost zero students to showings of *If You Love This Planet* and discussions of *The Fate of the Earth*.

I was terrified in those days. I pored over maps that depicted potential blast zones if Toronto were ever the target of a nuclear weapon. I was a strange and morbid teenager, I know. You don't have to tell me.

That was not even the connection I wanted to discuss with Setsuko. We talked a bit more about the new international nuclear ban treaty, and how she felt betrayed by Canada and Japan, which had not participated in the negotiations. Still, disarmament work had given her peace: she had fulfilled the promise to her friends and family killed by the bomb.

The bomb: There it was. I said, testing the ground, "So there's this strange connection between us..." Setsuko looked at me expectantly. I took a deep breath — I was crossing from my position as neutral journalistic observer, a position I've never been particularly good at maintaining, anyway — and told her my family's story.

"My grandfather worked at the mine that produced the uranium ore for the bomb." There, I said it. She looked at me with curiosity, but not horror. I told her the whole story—my maternal grandfather, Herman Mulvogue, was an accountant at Eldorado Mines at Great Bear Lake, NWT, where some of the uranium ore for the Manhattan Project was dug from the ground. He also worked at Eldorado's refinery in Port Hope, Ontario.

No one knew where the uranium was going, least of all my grandfather. He used to tell stories about American soldiers guarding the ore, with rifles pointed out at the bleak tundra. The Dene men who mined and carried the ore were never told of the dangers they faced from their toxic loads. It was shipped south and processed and sent to New Mexico, where it became part of the most dangerous weapon the world would ever know. A weapon that tore apart Setsuko Nakamura's world when it exploded above city like "a sheet of sun," as *The New Yorker*'s John Hersey described it in a famous article.

My grandfather was lovely, gentle, and learned—a deeply thoughtful man who struggled with alcoholism most of his life. He taught himself the Japanese national anthem, and would sing it to us. Why? I have no idea. I wish he were alive to talk about it, but he died when I was twelve. I think he and Setsuko would have liked each other. He was one tiny cog in a giant machine, a machine made of millions of human cogs and gears that stretched from northern Canada to Japan. The role he played was inconsequential. Most of the uranium for the bomb ending up being imported from the Belgian Congo anyway.

Still, we are tied across history, Setsuko and I. I finished telling her the story and she looked at me for a minute and said, finally, "What fate!" I don't believe in fate, though. I never have. I don't think she does, either, really: She has always been furious with people who suggest that God spared her life because he had a special purpose for her. What did that say about the people who were melted that day? Did they have no special purpose?

I helped Setsuko put the cherries back in the fridge. She had to save her strength for the Hiroshima anniversary celebration that was quickly approaching. It was held every year at Toronto's Peace Garden, a garden she was instrumental in building.

A few days after we met, she sent me a note, thanking me for my visit, expanding on her thoughts on disarmament, and reflecting on the story I told her about my grandfather: "I tremble with the thought," she wrote. "Two innocent human beings become connected totally by chance in the larger scheme of life."

It made me tremble, too. The world is a random place, full of chaos and chance: This has always been my view of the universe, which is both wildly terrifying and oddly comforting. Because if there is no fate, no grand plan, then all we have to fall back upon is the ingenuity and resilience of the human project. The comfort we can bring each other in the eye-blink we have together. The things we can make, and share.

Every time I interview someone I come away enriched; I can never predict which impressions will linger. It's the intelligence and courage that Phyllis James talked about, and the damn-the-torpedoes fieriness of Germaine Greer, the doggedness and brilliance of Hilary Mantel, and Setsuko Thurlow's determination to insist on speaking for the dead who cannot. Every one of them was a teacher, and I was lucky to listen and learn, if only for a brief moment.

A VIEW FROM THE OUTSIDE:
A LETTER TO MY YOUNGER SELF

Dear Young Liz,

Look at you — only twenty-two years old and you've
got a desk at Canada's national newspaper. A full-time
job. Yes, you're too afraid to ask anyone where the bath-
room is, and you're anxiously chain-smoking your way
to the pulmonary ward. But you're doing it.

As a copy editor, your job is to smooth the stories
that come your way, to find errors and fix them. You
try to write funny headlines on funny stories, serious
headlines on stories about war and death. When you
accidentally put a typo into the very first headline you
write for the paper, you will go home and cry, and then

drown your sorrows with your boyfriend, the budding alcoholic. You will be grateful that a senior editor caught the mistake before the paper was printed. You will come back to work again the next day, head down, and open a new story to edit.

Sometimes, you'll be required to call the reporters and ask questions about their stories: This will take more nerve than calling strangers. This newspaper is the voice of Canada's establishment, and its writers are experts in their fields, experienced, battle-hardened — and, as it turns out, very affable. Most of them are men, though this is changing. Almost all of them are white.

This will not strike you as odd. In 1989, the country's media landscape looks like the Prairies after a winter storm, featureless in its whiteness. There are exceptions, of course, but they are too few. The number of Black, Brown, Asian, or Indigenous reporters or on-air personalities is tiny. The country's schisms are still taught along historical and linguistic lines, English and French.

And, shamefully, this won't bother you very much. You don't even really notice. You pass as one of the token ethnics at the WASPY picnic. The vowel at the end of your name makes you distinct from the Mcs and Macs who fill the pages of the newspaper; you are duskier than just about everybody else. When a story about the mafia in Toronto enters the editing system and someone jokingly suggests "Give it to Renzetti," you'll laugh along with the rest of the editors. It's just easier that way.

Besides, you are too hung up on issues of sexism to notice the presence of racism. Feminism is your cause, and you seek out the older female journalists at the paper, some of whom will become mentors. They too are all white. You are ready to fight one injustice only: You don't see that injustice is a web, and that all exploitations are strung together, and that in many, many ways you are more fortunate than most. You won't realize it for decades to come.

When you've been at the paper for four years, a Men's column will be introduced. Seriously. A column about men, as if the whole paper were not already run by men, its pictures taken by male photographers, its stories sourced with male voices. You will be filled with rage, which is pretty much your default mood anyway.

You will propose a rebuttal, and will be surprised when they agree to publish it. You will write about systemic discrimination against women, about violence, about the inevitable backlash "when women show the audacity to reach for men's privilege pie." Astoundingly, the newspaper will decide to give you your own column, which won't run for very long but will increase the size of your own privilege pie. Unfortunately, you'll still be a little bit too dim-witted and self-absorbed to see it that way. You will continue to operate from a position of grievance, and fail to recognize those whose list of reckonings is much longer than yours. It's hard to give up the position of most-trod-upon.

Fast forward a couple of decades, and picture how your life has changed. The scales have started to fall from your eyes — slowly, again, but you're middle-aged. Nothing on your body moves as fast as it used to. The concept of "white feminism" as a discriminatory dynamic has surfaced over the years and caused a defensive backlash among — not surprisingly — white feminists. The work of self-examination is tricky and fraught, and you are perhaps too enamoured with your own oppression to carry out the necessary repairs.

Your newspaper will start to post videos in an effort to expand its audience, and one in particular will catch your attention: A young Canadian political activist, Brittany Amofah, speaks on the issue of white feminism, which she defines as "a feminism that is exclusionary and discriminates against women of colour." She says that, as a Black woman, she had been reluctant to call herself a feminist, because the movement pushed away people like her — as well as women of different sexualities and classes. But now she's decided she can effect change from within: "I want to showcase that feminism looks very different to different people, and that it's important to hear and understand the voices of women of colour."

One hot summer evening you'll be sitting with a friend and colleague, Hannah Sung, listening to the brilliant American writer Roxane Gay talk about *Hunger*, her new memoir about the aftermath of trauma. It is an intimate and raw book that pulls you under like the sea.

You can only imagine how difficult it is for Gay, a self-admittedly shy person, to speak about the book every night. But she does, gamely and hilariously. At the end of the evening there is a question-and-answer session. The crowd is made largely of young women, and they hurry toward the microphones. There are questions about the writing process, Gay's family, pop culture. One woman comes forward—you can't see her, you're up in the balcony—and asks Gay, in essence, what feminism must do to be more responsive to women of colour.

Gay shifts on the sofa on stage. She has thought about this question a lot, to put it mildly. She says: "In the past, white Feminism—feminism with a capital *F*—tended to ignore any woman who is not white, heterosexual, able, and middle class. That's frustrating.

In my experience, the only way to be intersectional is to be intersectional. If people won't get on board, they aren't part of your world, or your feminism. They get left behind.

"It's frustrating that we still have to start at *A*, and we never seem to move past *B*, and we need to be at *E*. I wish I had a better answer. But honestly, *we* don't have to do anything. White women have to do something."

That statement will be greeted with thunderous applause. You will look over at Hannah as the applause subsides, and you'll want to talk about it, but then it will occur to you with something like a slap: Hannah has already done the work. She has produced a terrific, award-winning podcast about race called Colour Code along with another talented colleague, Denise Balkissoon. They have done the challenging work of trying to sort out Canada's complex attitudes toward race. I'm not sure either of them needs more hand-wringing questions about where we go from here.

A couple of months later, you'll be at the Women in the World Summit in Toronto, a kind of Femapalooza organized by editor Tina Brown. On stage there is a procession of women telling important stories from around the world—from Iran, Cambodia, the Middle East, and the United States, where racial wounds are as raw as ever. The women are Black, Brown, Asian,

Indigenous, queer. The audience is almost all white. It does not escape your attention that, once again, you're sitting and listening while someone else does the work.

One of the speakers, Tamika Mallory, is a lifelong activist for racial justice and one of the cofounders of the Women's March on Washington. Mallory is speaking on the subject of "bro culture," but she takes a moment to connect the dots for those who are too clueless, or unwilling, to see for themselves. She brings up the important and increasingly well-known research of UCLA law professor Kimberlé Crenshaw on the subject of intersecting power structures and exploitation:

"Sexism, racism, Islamophobia, all the other isms that you can think of, they're all happening at the same time and not in a vacuum," Mallory says. "All of these issues are coming together and each one of us being impacted by all of them. We have to be willing to speak up on behalf of others that might be dealing with issues that we're not concerned with. If you are concerned about racism because perhaps you have an interracial child, you also have to lend your voice to the issue as it relates to sexism.

"We know across the world people are dealing with so many layers of isms that oppress them. We all have to be ready to add our voices, lend our dollars and our time and expertise to fighting back in intersectional ways, and to be our brother and sister's keeper. Acting like we don't know is not okay."

Roxane Gay and Tamika Mallory and Brittany Amofah have been doing the work, along with all the other women from marginalized communities. They live the reality of injustice every day, and then are expected to mop up our tears. We continue to ask them to do the work for us—to tell us what to read, how to be better, how to absolve our guilt. But that's not their burden anymore; it's ours.

When you talk to young feminists, you'll see that they understand this instinctively. Your middle-aged white friends, still annoyed by everyday battles with idiots, will find it a harder lesson to absorb: We never got to have our moment, and now we're expected to give it up! The lessons will be dark and painful. One day, you'll interview a young Canadian feminist, a journalist named Lauren McKeon who wrote an illuminating book called *F-Bomb: Dispatches from the War on Feminism*. She understands the threat to the movement comes from outside—from the familiar forces of oppression—but also from within, as the movement fails to accommodate new voices and struggles to overcome its barriers of race and class. When you ask her what can be done, she has some simple answers:

"It's about elevating other voices, raising other

people's platforms. It can be as simple as turning down a guest spot on a panel in favour of somebody who hasn't been elevated. Or saying, 'I'll do it as long as these other voices are also represented,' so you don't get another all-white panel of a certain age. It's just listening more. We don't need to be so scared of losing our own platforms. Making room for other voices doesn't mean we won't be heard."

And that will prove to be the most difficult lesson to absorb. It may be hard to imagine, as a twenty-two-year-old with a chip on your shoulder about being a penniless girl with a funny surname, but there will come a time when you have to pass over the grievance microphone. The thing you'll realize, when you're middle-aged and sprouting hair in odd places, is that this will be harder than you can imagine. It's cathartic to stand in the spotlight and scream about injustice. You have fought for that place; why can't someone else give up their place instead?

But there are other women with different voices, different stories, different things to protest, and—this is the killer—their voices will be fresher and more interesting than yours. That's a kick in the teeth. You'll be required to question your assumptions. To search for new books and sources of information to fill in the gaps in your embarrassing lack of knowledge. And you'll often fail, because you're as much a loud-mouthed ego-maniac as the next person. Possibly worse. But at least you will learn to try harder. Because if you don't, this movement you love so much will fail—and it will collapse from within.

Good luck with being twenty-two. One day, someone will show you the way to the washroom.

Yours in solidarity,
Older Liz

THE LONG CRAWL TO DEFEAT, THE SLOW MARCH TO VICTORY

IT WAS THE sight of the girl in the prisoner's uniform that stopped me. At that point, I'd been wandering around the Donald Trump rally in Florida for an hour, past grown men yelling "Trump that bitch" and "Lock her up." I'd paused to look at a miniature Hillary Clinton puppet, lovingly crafted to hideous effect, locked in a cage. I'd touched the cotton of a T-shirt that showed cartoon Trump urinating on the word "Hillary."

I'd been inoculated, in other words. After wading through the toxins of the 2016 U.S. presidential campaign, the venomous exhalations of a sick body politic, I thought nothing could surprise me. And then I saw the girl.

She was standing on the green hillside of the MidFlorida Credit Union Amphitheatre, bathed in the rich glow of the late October Florida sun. All around her people were wearing Trump shirts, Trump hats, Trump socks. But the girl's outfit trumped them all. She was dressed as an imprisoned Hillary Clinton. That is, she wore a striped prisoner's uniform on her body and a rubber Hillary Clinton mask on her face. If there were any doubt about the message we were meant to take away, she also wore a button that said "Lock Her Up."

A small crowd surrounded the girl, laughing and pointing and taking pictures. At first, I thought, *That can't be a child in there. It has to be a very tiny, very angry adult.* Although I'd just spent the past few days interviewing Floridians, many of them women, who told me that Hillary Clinton was a liar, a murderer, and a literal demon, I couldn't wrap my neurons around this level of hostility. Who would suggest to their daughter that the first female candidate with an actual chance to win the presidency was not only unqualified for the job, but deserved to be imprisoned for having the gall to run?

There was a woman standing by the girl's side, smiling at the attention. This must be mom. Mom, and likely Dad, too, would have arranged this spectacle. Let's be generous to them and say that this Imprisoned

Hillary idea was all the child's. She woke up one morning, put down her Baby-Sitters Club book and turned off Snapchat, and decided: *Hell, I'm going to the Trump rally tonight dressed as Lock Her Up!*

Even so, someone gave her the idea that Hillary Clinton — former Secretary of State, lawyer, feminist, advocate for children of this girl's age — was not a person qualified to run for president, or in fact a person at all but rather an object of hatred and contempt.

I looked at her beaming mother and made a vague gesture with my phone. Sure, the mother nodded. Go ahead and take a picture of my daughter in her grotesque rubber mask, her two small thumbs held cheerily aloft. I took a couple of pictures, the little girl framed against the green grass and the piercing blue of Florida's sky.

"It looks like a Diane Arbus photo," a friend would later say.

My journalistic instincts abandoned me. I should have interviewed the mother and the daughter, asked them why they were there, who had poisoned the well they drink from. But I didn't. I felt sick to my stomach, for the first time since I started following the campaign closely at its beginning. I felt like I was witnessing the mistrust and fear that women are taught about other women, and keep stored in their bones and their muscles, and deny even to themselves and pass on to their daughters.

The girl hugged her mother, turned away, and peeled off her rubber mask. It must have been stifling in there. Her long blonde hair tumbled out, and she immediately began to turn cartwheels on the grass, her prisoner's stripes a pinwheeled blur. I imagined Hillary herself peeling off her mask at the end of the day, putting it in a drawer marked Campaign Bullshit, and sitting down for a stiff Scotch and a Louise Penny novel.

I imagined my daughter, who was eleven and looked like this girl, although her hair was long and dark, not blonde. She was back home in Toronto. I bought her a Clinton campaign T-shirt that said "I'm With Her," but she would never end up wearing it because by the time I gave it to her the world had gone off a cliff. The T-shirt would sit folded on her shelf, a reminder of a wound too painful to revisit.

My daughter kept the T-shirt, in the same way that I'd kept men's shirts after they'd broken my heart, as a reminder of the way that life is torn and mended again. Maybe I'm just as bad as Prisoner Hillary's mom, using my child as a billboard for my political beliefs. My daughter, too, absorbed the prevailing winds in our household: She echoed back my feminism. Did it come from within her, or was she just parroting what she knew I wanted to hear?

The rally was about to begin. On stage, a wizened relic talked about God and, inevitably, making America great again. The crowd seemed equally divided between men and women.

I was particularly interested in how women could bring themselves to vote for Trump, who, at this point, had been accused of sexual groping by twelve women. They had all come forward after the release of his infamous *Access Hollywood* tape, in which he bro'd down with TV presenter Billy Bush over the many benefits of stardom. According to the future president, a female target would allow a famous man to grab her "by the pussy." Later, Trump dismissed this statement—which seemed tantamount to acknowledging sexual assault—as "locker room talk."

The female Trump supporters I talked to were on his side: They repeated his excuse, using the phrase "locker room talk." They said it all happened long in the past. Astonishingly, many of them also echoed Trump's insinuation that the women making the allegations were too unattractive to warrant his attention. "Have you seen Melania?" one of them asked, eyebrow raised meaningfully. I felt like I was trapped in a surreal dimension where we'd all been given the same puzzle pieces, but my jigsaw showed a giraffe while theirs showed a crocodile.

The crocodile, to these women, was Hillary Clinton. I was unprepared for the depth of hatred and vitriol among a certain segment of the population. I thought I'd find it among men, but they were actually smart enough to cloak their misogyny in a bland layer of inoffensive language. Before the rally in Tampa, I approached one elderly lady, her snowy hair piled on her head, to ask her opinion of Clinton. I'd barely opened my mouth when she leaned in and said, "She's a liar, liar, liar, liar, liar." Her cheery old face contorted with bitterness. Her friend turned to her, in an effort to lighten the mood, and whispered, "Remember you haven't taken your blood pressure medication yet."

Another woman at the rally, a nurse and an immigrant from Central America herself— "But legal, okay?"— told me that Clinton was a murderer, and a demon. Oddly, this did not surprise me. What did surprise me was how little had changed since 1872, when Victoria Woodhull, the first woman to seek the American presidency, was known in the press as "Mrs. Satan."

It is one thing to recognize, on a theoretical level, the depth of hatred levelled at Clinton. It was quite another to experience it, in your ears and eyes, and

on your skin. It was the difference between watching
a slasher movie and being followed home yourself by
a crazed killer. What shocked me the most, though it
shouldn't because I am a feminist who has been writing
about this stuff for decades, is that some of the loudest
voices around me were women's. *Internalized misogyny,*
I wanted to whisper to the women in front of me, sitting with her daughters, all wearing pink Women for
Trump shirts: *It's called internalized misogyny, sisters.*

By the time Trump reached the stage, following
a cavalcade of minor Floridian celebrities, the crowd
was near the boil, the lid rattling on a stew of glee and
resentment. It did not take long for him to turn the heat
up: "The best evidence that the system is rigged is the
fact that Hillary Clinton, despite her many crimes, was
even allowed to run for president in the first place." It
was the crowd's cue to begin the chant they'd heard
at every Trump rally when they'd turn on the news:
"Lock her up! Lock her up!" Trump prowled the stage,
patting his soft, white hands together, beaming encouragement. "Lock her up!" I wondered if the little girl in
the Hillary costume was chanting along, caught up
in the wave, thrilled to be among the adults and their
delicious hate.

On the way out, the crowd was giddy and spent, collectively in need of a post-coital cigarette. I was reeling:

I didn't see Prisoner Hillary anywhere; perhaps her parents had taken her home. It was a school night, after all.

ON ELECTION DAY, back home in Toronto, I phoned my mother. She was, to put it mildly, a Hillary superfan: I admired Clinton for her ambition and savvy, for her policy commitments that would improve women's lives, but I also recognized her limitations. I had seen, first-hand, that there were Americans whose loathing of her was visceral, if not entirely rational. My mother's affection existed on a whole other level. In Florida I bought her a pink Clinton cap that said "Stronger Together." I imagined her asking to be buried in it.

When Clinton won the presidential nomination, the first woman to secure the candidacy for a major political party, my mother wept. I jokingly told her that she hadn't been that emotional at the births of her eight grandchildren; she didn't correct me.

My mother, a progressive to the core and a political junkie, was born twelve years after women in Canada won the right to vote. There was one woman sitting in Canada's parliament in the year of her birth. Mildred remembered not being able to own her own credit card. She had seen me climb, and my sister. She had seen the world turn its face toward progress. And now there was a chance that Clinton would shatter "the highest and hardest glass ceiling."

So when I phoned her on the morning of the election, I expected joy and anticipation. Instead, I heard trepidation. "How do you think it's going to go?" she asked.

"I think she's going to win."

"*Mmmm*," said my mother, in the same tone she used to judge a dubious dress colour. I felt the first hint of anxiety. Mildred had also seen the world turn away from progress; a history of adversity was buried in her bones.

But the signs, that day, were good. Social media filled with pictures of women in their pantsuits, with babies in pantsuits, drag queens in pantsuits. A live camera showed the steady stream of voters making a pilgrimage to Susan B. Anthony's grave in Rochester, placing their "I Voted" stickers on the headstone. In 1872 Anthony was fined $100 for trying to vote in the presidential election to protest the fact that "the blessings of liberty are forever kept from women and their female posterity." She never paid the fine.

My finger grew weary from refreshing my Twitter feed: I couldn't get enough of its photos of women voting, elated and beaming. My feed was a stream of affirmation of what I already believed, which was of course a problem. I swam in a filter bubble of my own making — a dangerous thing for a person, more dangerous for a journalist. I'd been listening to voices that chimed in glorious harmony with mine, and forgotten about the child in Tampa in her prisoner's costume.

I had also put out of my mind an article I'd read in the *Washington Post* a couple of weeks earlier, which carried the headline "How sexism drives support for Donald Trump." In it, three political scientists from the University of Michigan wrote that their research into voters' attitudes showed that "sexism was strongly and significantly correlated with support for Trump." At that point, Trump voters were thought to be driven by fear — of poverty, of job loss, of a changing America — but the political scientists' analysis showed that fury was a much more potent fuel: "Our research suggests that the role of racial prejudice or sexism may be catalyzed more by anger." There was a rage monster lying dormant in America. I had witnessed it, but I was too blind to see.

That evening, I sent my daughter and son off to see *Matilda*, the musical based on Roald Dahl's vision of a world ruined by adults' cruelty. My son, a political obsessive like his grandmother and an American by birth, kept his eye on the exit polls. My daughter just wanted to know if she'd wake up to a historic dawn:

"When will we know?" she asked at the door. "When will we know if she's won?"

I finished writing the piece my editors had asked for, about the historic significance of the first female presidency. I honed it, and edited it, and hit send. Here's how it began, the piece that would never see the light of day:

"In the end, she was the right woman after all. Despite the endless criticism aimed her way, Hillary Clinton did not smile too much or too little, she was neither too tough nor too frail, and it didn't matter if anyone wanted to have a beer with her. What mattered is that millions of Americans judged her singularly fit to run their country."

I wasn't the only one who had to throw my words in the garbage. Later, much later, Clinton would reveal the contents of the acceptance speech she would have given if she'd become president, standing in her white suffragette's pantsuit with all the shattered glass at her feet.

She would have thanked her mother, Dorothy, who died in 2011 at the age of ninety-two. Clinton often cited her mother, survivor of a dreadful childhood, as a source of strength and inspiration. In her speech, she would have addressed her mother, who'd been abandoned at the age of eight and sent to live with uncaring grandparents. She would have told Dorothy that her misery would give way to happiness eventually: "And as hard as it might be to imagine, your daughter will grow up and become president of the United States."

The prospect of a Clinton presidency grew dimmer by the moment. I channelled my bewilderment into a tweet: "What are we going to tell our daughters?" No one had an answer, least of all me: When my daughter came home, I couldn't bear to tell her the truth, so I lied and said that we didn't know.

I woke my mother when I called. She had gone to bed, disconsolate, and here I was disrupting her ancient, patchwork sleep.

"Do we know yet?" she asked, her voice quiet.

"It doesn't look good," I said.

She sighed, and click, she was gone.

I wanted to punch the world, for her sake. Hadn't she earned some good news? Was the universe destined to be ruled by assholes forever? I couldn't bear to stay up and watch Trump's acceptance speech. I went back to my bottle of whisky; I was halfway through. And then I dragged myself off to bed and had bad dreams; whisky or life gave me nightmares or perhaps a bit of both.

Clinton never got to make her acceptance speech, of course; she never got to thank Dorothy. Instead, the next morning, she appeared before the cameras in New York to address her supporters. She was wearing a purple blouse, a conciliatory gesture—the red states and the blue as one—but I couldn't imagine conciliation was much on her mind. She looked exhausted. Everyone in my world was heavy with grief. How was Clinton holding it together?

I managed to hold it together, watching the speech on TV, until she said: "And to all the little girls who are watching this, never doubt that you are valuable and powerful and deserving of every chance and opportunity in the world to pursue and achieve your own dreams."

I phoned my mother again. As soon as she picked up, I burst into tears. She listened to my blubbering for a moment, and then she said, "I've got to go. *The View*'s coming on and I want to hear what Whoopi has to say." Later that evening, when I phoned her again, she said drily: "Have you stopped crying yet?" It was her greatest gift to me, this flintiness at her core, the rock-hard centre that survived every natural disaster life threw at her.

After Clinton had finished speaking, I sat down to write a new column, seeking answers to the question that I'd asked the previous night: What would we tell our daughters? The words gushed forth, an unstoppable fountain of rage. "For the daughters out there, the time for fighting is at hand. It is now perhaps apparent that our mothers and grandmothers did not win every battle, and the ground they did win is slipping away under our feet. Instead of being discouraged, go and put on your Nasty Woman T-shirt and engage in the battle, in defiance of the sexism that lies like a freshly woken monster in your path. In the words of the old protest song: 'Take it easy, but take it.'"

It felt cathartic, and I hit send. My tiny bit of light in the world. In truth, though, those brave words felt as flimsy as the newsprint they were printed on. The monster was alive in the world; it would never rest; it would never give up its power.

When I picked up my daughter at her after-school club, she told me that she and her friends had spent the day talking about Trump's victory. They were blessedly ignorant of electoral college votes and swing states and email servers and a far-off place called Benghazi, but, in the manner of eleven-year-olds everywhere, they understood bullies and were deeply concerned with fairness.

She put on her seatbelt, and I put on my game face. I told her that history was on our side, even though I didn't much believe it myself. I told her that America would have a woman president in her lifetime, that Canada would elect another female prime minister.

"Sure," she said, turning to look out the car window. "In 55,000 years."

IT TOOK LESS than 55,000 years for a sliver of light to pierce the hate-dark clouds. Two and a half months after the election I emerged from L'Enfant Plaza subway station onto the wide boulevards of Washington, D.C. Outside the subway I was swept along like a cork in a current, part of a vast, happy-angry crowd, a crowd of hundreds of thousands that jammed the streets of America's capital. It was the day after Trump's lacklustre inauguration, but no one was talking about that because all eyes had turned to this momentous gathering, the Women's March on Washington.

I was pressed on all sides by old women carrying signs that said "I Can't Believe I Still Have to Protest This Shit" and young women chanting "This Is What Democracy Looks Like." The crowd was rosy with pink knitted pussy hats, the Phrygian caps of the new revolution.

A toddler sat on her dad's shoulders, wearing a tiny white shirt that said "This is what a feminist looks like." He must have bought it for her, ordering it off a website, perhaps, with deliberation and bottled rage, in the same way that Inmate Hillary's parents had prepared her costume in Tampa. Was that just a couple of months before? It seemed like years.

Ahead of me, a young woman carried a sign that she had painted herself: "I stopped counting at 44," it said on one side, and on the other, "Black lives still matter." Erin was thirty, marching with her mother, who had never been to a protest before. (This was a common theme; many of the people I talked to over the course of the day were demonstrating for the first time, and many of them were with mothers, sisters, aunts.)

"As a Black woman I don't feel safe at the moment," Erin said. "It's important that we show up, and tell the world that it's not okay for our president to be racist, sexist, and xenophobic."

Erin, it occurred to me, was the future; her mother was the future. They knew, as Americans, what protest can do to improve their lives. The crowd filled all the wide spaces between the museums of the Smithsonian complex. Those museums — temples of knowledge, free to the public, endowed for eternity — are the highest ideals of America made manifest. Inside, they provide testament to the place of protest at the heart of that country's democracy: At the Museum of American History, the Woolworths lunch counter, site of the Greensboro protest sit-in, stands across the hall from the wagon that delivered the suffragette newspaper *The Woman's Daily*. Every victory for social justice had been hard-won in a relentless ground war. This was one more skirmish, not the end.

On that grey day in January, the Women's March on Washington earned a place in the Hall of Fame of protests. It began on Facebook, in the despairing, weepy hours after the election. It was born there, a seed, but it grew into something surpassing everyone's wildest expectations. Organizers had hoped that 200,000 might show up; instead, more than 500,000 brought the capital to a standstill. They arrived from all over the country, some from across the world, in fury and determination. Over the course of the day, social media overflowed with pictures of sister protests around the world, from tiny ones in Jos, Nigeria, and Sandy Cove, Nova Scotia, to a wintry slog in Haines, Alaska, where marchers were bent double against the wind and snow.

Yet, despite the fury that propelled us, there was a particular spirit I could only think of as female, for better or worse. No one misbehaved. Everyone brought lots of water. Energy bars were unpeeled, shared, the wrappers placed carefully in pockets for disposal later.

Under a concrete overhang, I found another mother and daughter, Fawzia and Shaza, who were also marching for the first time. Shaza was a high-school senior in neighbouring Alexandria, Virginia. They had come to express their solidarity with other women. Shaza said that they were anxious about the possibility of a Muslim registry—a policy reportedly considered by the Trump team during the election. They didn't think it would come to pass.

In fact, she said, people at the march had come up to her to say "*As-salāmu alaykum*" and compliment her on her pale blue hijab. The teenager had a message for the new president, which pretty much summed up the mood of the day: "I'm a citizen. I was born here. It's as much my country as it is his."

I slipped further into the crowd, threading my way between bodies, trying to get closer to the stage where feminist heroes of the past and future echoed Shaza's message: This is our country, our day, our time. We will not watch the clock roll back. As I listened, I felt lightness in my frozen feet, my frozen heart.

Sound bounced off the walls and the bodies: Gloria Steinem was on stage, though I couldn't get near enough to see her. I could hear her, though, and later I would watch her on YouTube, a lioness in a red scarf and tinted glasses: "Because this, *this*, is the upside of the downside. This is an outpouring of energy and true democracy like I have never seen in my very long life. It is wide in age. It is deep in diversity."

The lineup of speakers *was* deep in diversity. The march's organizers had listened to criticism, early on, that the day could not be constrained by white feminists. To do so would not just be short-sighted and unjust, it would mean failure. The women traditionally pushed to the margins by the historical forces of oppression could not be pushed there by the sisterhood as well. They needed to be at the centre, working the gears and levers, holding the microphones, making the speeches.

Never mind that women of colour had earned their place at the head of the resistance: 94 percent of Black women and 68 percent of Latinas voted for Clinton. On the other hand, astoundingly, 53 percent of white women voted for Trump, choosing tribalism and self-interest over the common good. As Michelle Obama would later say, "Any woman who voted against Hillary Clinton voted against their own voice."

The author and transgender activist Janet Mock took the stage to talk about the challenging work ahead: "Our movements require us to do more than just show up and say the right words," she said. "It requires us to break out of our comfort zones and be confrontational. It requires us to defend one another when it is difficult and dangerous." She was at the march, she said, to be "my sister's keeper." The young women around me put their pussy-hatted heads back and howled in agreement. Adrian, a college freshman standing by my side, waved the sign she carried; it was a middle finger raised to the world, except the finger was the symbol for the female gender turned upside down.

"Nice sign," I said.

"My girlfriend made it," Adrian replied. She was at the march with five college friends. They'd started crying on election night. It took a while to pick themselves up. She looked numb and exhausted.

As I stood and listened for four hours, a feeling of strangeness descended on me, a discombobulation. By the time a preternaturally poised six-year-old named Sophie Cruz, the daughter of undocumented immigrants, took the stage to talk about human rights in Spanish and English, I had located my sense of disconnect. We'd been listening to girls and women all day. For hours on end. From the Mothers of the Movement, speaking about their sons killed by police, to Angela Davis and her unashamed takedown of the "heteropatriarchy," they'd all been women's voices.

It set me rocking on my heels. When was the last time I listened to women speak, uninterrupted, for hours on end—about labour rights and social justice and race relations? When was the last time I listened to women speaking uninterrupted about *anything*? I thought of my daughter, at home, and how often I had to tell her father and brother to be quiet and let her finish a thought.

It felt radically female, as if hundreds of thousands of menstrual cycles might spontaneously synchronize right there outside the National Air and Space

Museum. In spite of the chaos of the day — no one
seemed to know where anything was, or in which direction we should move — a spirit of co-operation ruled.
In the weeks before the march, I'd rolled my eyes at
some of the rules imposed on participants. There could
be no pickets with wooden handles. No purses larger
than a few inches square. No bicycles. No backpacks,
unless they were transparent. Who owns a transparent backpack?

Apparently, a lot of women. Or at least they managed to find some. Thousands of transparent backpacks,
as far as the eye could see: All day long, I peered into
the secret lives of strangers, at their water bottles and
snack bars, their extra sweaters and books. It was a
revolution organized by the PTA.

I turned and join the stream of people marching
toward the White House, along the broad boulevards
where in 1913 suffragettes marched and were beaten
for their temerity, the day before Woodrow Wilson's
inauguration. That was a turning point in the history
of women's rights; perhaps this would be, too.

For a while I walked alongside Casey, a transgender
army veteran, and her wife, Karen, who were seriously
considering a move to Canada. Casey's sign showed an
American flag upside-down, a military signal of dis-
tress. I could see a pack of Kools in her transparent

backpack: I was tempted to ask her for one. As we walked and talked, a man came alongside, pointing to Casey's sign identifying her as a veteran. "Thank you for your service," he said.

"Does that happen all the time?" I asked.

She nodded. "There's a lot of good people in this country. You just have to look for them."

I left Casey and Karen and found myself under a giant cardboard cut-out of Hillary Clinton carried by a group of young men and women, who giggled as they shifted the candidate from hand to hand. Clinton herself did not attend the protest. Later, she would say that she didn't want to distract from the march's message.

That, instead, was left to Madonna, who yelled from the stage that the new president could "suck a dick." Madonna at full Madonnosity made me laugh, as did the woman holding aloft a picture of Vladimir Putin wearing a tiny "I Voted" sticker in his lapel. It was a hell of a lot better to laugh than to cry. It was better to march than to lie in a soggy heap wondering why the lights had gone out.

At the end of the day, my feet exhausted, I paused to marvel at how quickly the women of America went from crying to organizing, from fretting to fighting. Historically, organizing has been our role: We make phone calls and arrange billets and photocopy the flyers and take our places next to the men who raise their fists on the podiums. Not on this day, though. This day belonged to us.

ANOTHER CARDBOARD CUT-OUT of Hillary Clinton. What are the chances? Nine months after the Women's March, I brought my mother to a convention centre in downtown Toronto to hear Clinton speak. Mildred applied crimson lipstick while we waited for the event to begin. As she sidled up to cardboard Hillary to have her picture taken, her smile was bright, if slightly forced. This was my gift to my mother; I couldn't change the world, but I could shell out $160 to make her pretend, for an hour, that everything would be okay in the end.

It had been a hard eleven months since the election of the man my mother would refer to only as "that buffoon." If anything, those eleven months had been worse than we imagined—the president ordered a controversial travel ban on people from several Muslim-majority countries, which was repeatedly challenged in court; he refused to condemn lethal racist behaviour; his administration rolled back wage protection for women; reproductive rights were threatened across the country.

On the day I wrote this, a new poll revealed that 56 percent of respondents felt that Trump was "not fit" to be president. Across America, the resistance was strong: Women were signing up to run for political office in record numbers.

Above our heads in the convention centre, a screen showed the cover of Clinton's memoir, *What Happened*, which had sold hundreds of thousands of copies in the weeks after its release. A video played, and in it Clinton quoted Dorothy Rodham: "My mother taught me that everybody needs a chance, and a champion. And I still hear her voice urging me to keep working and fighting for right no matter what."

The atmosphere was jubilant and defiant. All five thousand seats were sold. Women roamed the aisles with their daughters and friends, their sisters and colleagues, some wearing pantsuits, some wearing T-shirts that said "Nasty Woman" and "I'm With Her." There were so many women that they started to colonize the men's washroom, which frankly is a revolution I could get behind.

My mother was beside herself with anticipation, her cane drumming the floor. This was her Woodstock. The lights dimmed and the crowd let up an anticipatory roar, and I thought of all the people who were afraid to say out loud during the campaign that they were with her. I thought of the male journalists who continued to write that she should "go the fuck away."

My mother climbed slowly to her feet, dropping her cane on me in the process. Teetering, she clapped so loudly that I worried she would have a stroke and I would be exposed as the terrible daughter who never got First Aid training. Mildred wore a bright red dress, the same red as Clinton's jacket, a red that said "No, I have a better idea, why don't *you* go the fuck away."

Not that Mildred would ever say something so profane. Her strongest epithet, saved for moments of great irritation, is *Jesus, Mary, and Joseph.* This is why I was taken aback when she turned to whisper in my ear, after listening to Clinton outline the various barriers to her election, including Russian meddling, sexism, the FBI: "Wow. She really got screwed."

I told you my mother was wise. On stage, Clinton ran through the many reasons for her defeat, which also included a divided and rage-filled electorate and an overemphasis on her use of a personal email server. (She also accepted blame for the loss, although not as often in person as she had on the page; in her memoir, I counted more than twenty instances of regret or apology for her shortcomings during the campaign.)

And then there was, undeniably, sexism. Clinton didn't have time in her speech to go into all the ways that misogyny played a role in the campaign, because we needed to get home within the next century. She distilled one bit of research that Sheryl Sandberg shared with her: "For men, professional success and likeability go hand in hand. Not for women. The more successful a man becomes, the more people like him. With women it's the exact opposite. The more successful women become, the less people like us." She paused for a beat, with the timing of a sharpshooter: "I'm sure some women in this room have an inkling what I'm talking about."

"That's right," my mother said, nodding fiercely. I looked over at her, thinking that I knew nothing of her life, her struggles. What had she buried so deeply that she had forgotten, and I'll never know?

"So yes," Clinton continued, "there are lots of reasons why being a woman in politics can be downright infuriating." I remembered all that I had seen and heard during the election: the signs that showed Trump urinating on her name, the men yelling "Lock her up." I thought of the girl in her prisoner's uniform, outlined against the bright Florida sun.

Nothing would change until we made it change: "The only way to get sexism out of politics," Clinton said, her voice rising, the voice that was too shrill to be presidential, "is to get more women into politics." And the word "Yes" burst from my mother, as she climbed to her feet one more time.

KILLER ROBOTS, AMAZON PLANETS, AND THE FIGHT FOR THE FUTURE

IN THE SUMMER of 2017, a vending company called Three Square Market in River Falls, Wisconsin, held a "chip party." That is, it implanted microchips in fifty of its eighty employees. With their permission, of course. To make life easier, of course.

The radio frequency identification chip, just the size of one grain of rice, was implanted in each employee's hand, a procedure that was not in the least painful, according to Three Square Market's CEO, Todd Westby. He told CNBC that it felt like having someone step quickly on his hand while wearing a dress shoe. But there was so much to be gained for so little pain.

As CNBC noted, "The device allows door access to enter the building, [employees to] sign into their computer, and pay for snacks—all with a wave of their hand on a sensor. The microchip replaces passwords, ID badges, and even credit cards." The employees who got chipped were enthusiastic, Mr. Westby said: "The people that did decide to do it really were looking forward to the convenience that it does bring to the everyday life."

They were looking forward to the convenience. This might have been the moment when my trepidation about the future slid into full-blown panic. It's one thing to sign away your bodily autonomy, but it's quite another to barter it for faster access to a Sprite. Was convenience really now our Holy Grail? Had remembering passwords become too heavy a burden for our pleasure-seeking brains? Was this capitalism's end game—an army of microchipped drones passing in front of a vending machine or a door, too lazy even to reach into their own pockets? Had we reached the anthropological age called Can No Longer Be Bothered to Lift a Finger?

I would like to pretend to be cool with the whole microchipping idea. I would like to be the groovy futurist and not the thumbnail-chewing old lady who sees us hurtling toward hell in a handbasket. But I feel increasingly like Teddy, the main character in Kate Atkinson's incandescent novel *A God in Ruins*, a former bomber pilot who feels modern life spiralling beyond his control: "Like a dog, Teddy thought, he had had his day. 'I'm too old for the world,' he said."

Or is the world too fast for us? This moment, now, at the beginning of the twenty-first century, feels calamitous, perilous. I imagine it did for people at earlier moments of great technological change: *That mechanical loom, it's going to steal our Ned's job! I think I'll smash it flat with this here hammer.*

This moment feels particularly fraught, though. The last embers of capitalism's dying fire provide heat to fewer and fewer people, even as the oceans and skies grow hotter around us; technology proceeds at its own pace, untethered to morality, guided by a profit incentive unshared by most and understood by few. Social justice is still a mirage for those historically pushed to society's edges. Loneliness is a public health crisis. Market forces alone determine what we should and should not value, even as wealth inequality grows. Where is the vision for tomorrow?

IT NORMALLY COSTS twenty-four dollars for tourists to visit St. Paul's Cathedral, Christopher Wren's wondrous palace of God in Central London. On the balmy evening I visited in May 2012, it was free, which was ironic because we were there to talk about how pretty much everything in our lives had come to carry a price tag.

I rode the Tube from my home in North London to hear the Harvard political philosopher Michael Sandel speak about his book *What Money Can't Buy: The Moral Limits of Markets*. The world was still reeling from the banking collapse of 2008, and further unbalanced by the global Occupy movement that followed. It seemed the world was waking up every morning filled with doubt: *Where the hell were we going? Did you bring the map? Wait, I thought you brought the map!* Sandel's book, which beautifully synthesized the way that market thinking had come to dominate all facets of human life, blew the cobwebs from my mind. It marked the place where we were, and that place was terrifying.

"We have drifted from having a market economy to being a market society," Sandel told the packed audience, his voice echoing through the cathedral's soaring pillars. We sat together on folding chairs, the bearded and sensibly shod folk of the anxious middle gathered in a hallowed space that had hosted the funerals of queens and admirals. Frightened as we were, there were not a lot of people in that audience in danger of falling off the edge. That was Sandel's point.

"At a time of rising inequality, as money comes to

buy more and more, the effect is that rich and poor increasingly lead separate lives. There are fewer and fewer occasions, public spaces, where men and women from different walks of life encounter one another in the ordinary course of things." This, he said, would be corrosive to democracy in the end, because a society needed to have some sense of the common good as a goal for its members to work toward.

In a way, Sandel was preaching to the converted: He was just showing us new hymns. Money could buy everything at the beginning of the twenty-first century, if you had enough of it: New blood to replace your tired old blood; a fast-pass to bypass the crowds at the amusement parks and on the highways; advertising space on the forehead of a hungry college student. The market was our god, capitalism our church, and we worshipped whether we wanted to or not.

I wandered out into the velvet spring night—spring in Britain really is a delight beyond description—and walked across the cobblestones of St. Paul's churchyard. Here, a few months earlier, the raggedy tents of Occupy London had huddled against the Cathedral's stone walls. The church fathers had tried to banish them; the protesters hung on. I visited one day and talked to the protesters, who were damp but filled with frustrations ready to explode.

They were tired of cuts to public services, tired of greed, tired of the way the world was parcelled out by people they would never meet. They imagined something better, a happier way of living. Aaron, a twenty-year-old set painter, told me that his friends laughed at him for camping out in the cold and rain.

"It doesn't matter," he said. "This is a global awakening."

It felt, at that moment, as if there were a global awakening: that we had learned something from the legions of blank-eyed bankers shuffling like zombies from their towers, all their possessions in cardboard boxes. Maybe we had learned, finally, that the game was rotten from the inside.

Instead, the momentum seemed to fizzle. The Occupy movement was forced by state authority from its campsites, moving underground to feed into other social-justice streams. The banking collapse was forgotten, like a collective delusion, and neoliberalism continue to plough ahead, harnessing all human enterprise to the mechanism of markets. And instead of the great coming-together that Aaron mentioned, instead of the Age of Aquarius, we witnessed a great darkness descend. The Age of Sauron, more like.

I, an inherent optimist, felt my heart sag as I watched events unfold, a riot of discontent and fracture. The promise of the Arab Spring was squandered. Corruption and economic collapse in Brazil. Fascism alive and well in Europe and on the streets of America. A freshly engaged, terrifying nuclear arms race. A poisonous, poisoned demagogue in the White House. As women's reproductive rights were squashed across the United States, people watched *The Handmaid's Tale* on their TV screens, not noticing the reality of *The Handmaid's Tale* creeping up outside their windows. It was hardly comforting that this blinding and lethal ignorance is central to Margaret Atwood's prophetic novel. The mirror cracked. No one could bear to look into it.

I became fixated on the erosion of trust in public institutions, which seemed to me the precursor of a great fall. Every year, studies would show that people's trust in the established order was failing, and that they no longer believed in government, media, churches, business, the justice system. Worse, they actively mistrusted these institutions. Worse, this mistrust led them to believe life was getting worse, not better.

"There is growing despair about the future, a lack of confidence in the possibility of a better life for one's family." That sentence comes from the 2017 Edelman Trust Barometer, an annual report that polls residents in twenty-eight countries to determine their feelings about social institutions and governance. The title of the 2017 survey says it all: "Crisis in Trust." Trust in government, business, media, and NGOs had plummeted since the survey began in 2010. Fifty-three percent of respondents said the overall system had failed them; only fifteen percent believed it was working.

Clearly, money can't buy everything: It can't buy a system that works for most of the people. Or, perhaps more precisely, as presently constructed, the system is not one that most people can buy into. So where do we go from here? And is it up to women to fix a broken world? Let's just add that to our to-do list, shall we?

THE FIRST SEASON of the hilarious Canadian comedy program *Baroness von Sketch Show* contains a skit about what the future might look like if power changed at the top. It is the year 2050, and the setting is a World Summit held in Copenhagen. The camera reveals that all the participants are women.

"This is our first world summit since the revolution, where we ascended to power replacing our male counterparts," says the first woman to speak. She is not identified as the leader or the chair; clearly those hierarchical designations have fallen by the wayside. She asks if any delegates have had problems with their economies. The women shake their heads. Everything is fine. Climate concerns? Again, they agree it's all good.

"Conflict?" the woman at the podium asks. "Any war?"

The delegates chuckle, and one says "No, we just talk it out these days."

Finally, the representative from one region admits, slightly sheepishly, that she'd had a bit of conflict with another delegate: "Then I realized I was just projecting all my shit onto her." They grin at each other and link pinkies in solidarity.

Their business sorted in less than a minute, the women pack up their papers and prepare to leave. One of them says, "I can't believe this summit used to take days."

Bada-bing!

The sketch is genius for the way that it subtly undermines the notion of feminist utopia (we would *still* be blaming ourselves for any moment of conflict) while enforcing what many of us believe in our deepest hearts: The world would be a better place if women had more say in the running of things. At the very least it would be less fucked up.

When I was a child, the only imagined female future was the one we occasionally glimpsed on rainy Sundays when the Buffalo television station showed old science-fiction movies from the 1950s. There you'd seen planets run by women, cone-breasted and hair-sprayed. After initially making war on the square-jawed astronauts who invaded their planets, eventually they'd succumb to the charms of these earthlings whose manliness could barely be contained by their silver jumpsuits. With the arrival of the men, the women—who had until then been running around their planets without a care—would see the error of their unnatural ways. Then the future would be safe.

It is a truism that all imagined futures in some way embody the moment of their creation. In the postwar period, the patriarchy must have seen the first disquieting blips of female discontent on the radar; Betty Friedan was putting a name to this nameless anxiety. Consciousnesses were being raised at Formica tables across the land. No wonder men had to imagine other worlds in which their control was not only benign, but a salvation.

In 1976, Marge Piercy wrote her landmark futurist novel *Woman on the Edge of Time*. It's the story of a Mexican-American woman, Connie, who has suffered dire abuse at the hands of men and society, and ends up a tranquilized mess in a mental hospital. She is visited by Luciente, a woman from the year 2137, and shown a future free of oppression, where men and women live and love as they please, bound by no restrictions except that they do good for the community.

It is an idealized vision of the future, and a brave

one. Dystopias are more popular for writers than utopias, since they contain more drama and conflict. As novelists like to say, "Happiness writes white." Piercy chose a desperately tumultuous time to imagine a calmer and more just future.

The 1970s were a time of social upheaval and economic and political crises — yes, much like today. In this chaos, the seeds of feminism had taken hold and were blooming. There was serious progress advancing women's reproductive and economic freedom, a trajectory that was bound to continue till the great starburst of total equality and emancipation was reached. Or so it must have seemed at the time.

But, as Piercy writes in the preface to the fortieth-anniversary edition of *Woman on the Edge of Time*, that promise has not only not been fulfilled, it has in many ways been squandered: "Inequality has greatly increased. As I write this, more people are poor, more people are working two or three jobs just to get by, more people find that their savings and their future have been wiped out by bad health or losing their jobs." At the same time, women's political progress and control over their bodies has stalled or regressed. The result of the ascendance of corporatism, Piercy writes, is that we are too busy putting out today's fires to imagine how to spark a better future.

And then she notes something crucial: The way to understand a society and its progress is to look at the forces that control technology. "Who decides that trolleys and passenger trains are obsolete but that cars are all-important and our cities must be built around them as if they were the primary inhabitants?" she asks. "Who chooses which technology is explored? Who sets the rules for what is dangerous and what is acceptable risk?"

Who is setting the rules? This is a vital question. And here's another, which seems particularly pertinent: Have we agreed what the game should be? And if this one's fixed, can we start another? Would a future game designed by women be more fair? Would it at least be level enough so that all the paper money didn't drift to one side of the board?

LET'S RETURN TO Wisconsin for a moment, perhaps the least likely place for the dreams of technology to be made flesh. Soon, no part of the Earth will be immune from the reach of automation or artificial intelligence (AI). Should I say the "progress" of automation and AI, or the "creep"? Language is loaded; is this journey to human liberation or enslavement?

We've barely begun to consider these questions.

Robots, as it is often wearily pointed out, are not part of the future, they are part of the now. They perform surgery and drive trucks and compose symphonies and are much better at *Jeopardy!* than sausage-fingered humans. Those are the benign applications; some are more threatening. Unless we do something to regulate the advance of lethal autonomous weapons—that is, killer robots—they will entirely change the face of warfare.

This is quite apart from the worries about what automation will mean for our children's futures. A recent report from Ryerson University in Toronto predicted that more than 40 percent of jobs might disappear due to automation in the next ten to twenty years. It's the new generation of workers—people aged to fifteen to twenty-four—who will be most vulnerable to these changes. That's my kids, and your kids, or your neighbour's kids, if you happen to be child-free. These are the statistics that have me gasping awake every night, panicked, as if Vincent Vega just administered a hypodermic full of adrenalin to my heart.

We do not have the legislative or philosophical tools to even begin to contemplate this revolution. Bill Gates says we should place a tax on robot producers, and Elon Musk warns that AI must be regulated in some fashion. In the United States, there is a call for a Federal Robotics

Commission, which so far has not been heeded; the European Parliament in early 2017 called for a legislative framework to regulate the activity of robotics and AI. We may have left it a bit late. The cyborg horse may have already bolted the stable.

And if we can barely keep up with the latest shiny products being produced in Silicon Valley, how can we possibly pause to envisage a better future than the one we have now? Technology's advance is tied to the profit motive; we are too busy playing Candy Crush to imagine an alternative.

As the Israeli historian Yuval Noah Harari says in his book *Homo Deus: A Brief History of Tomorrow*: "The world is changing faster than ever before, and we are flooded by impossible amounts of data, of ideas, of promises and of threats. Humans are relinquishing authority to the free market, to crowd wisdom and to external algorithms partly because we cannot deal with the deluge of data."

I wish this didn't fill me with bowel-liquefying anxiety, but it does. I read the words of the cyber-utopians and transhumanists, with their promise of a gender-free future in which our brains will be uploaded into a central matrix for all eternity, amen, but I see no possibility of a better tomorrow until we address the crushing inequalities of the present. I personally do not want immortality in a world where some people are still split-shift wage slaves and others piss in gold toilets.

I apologize for being such a bitter pessimist. I'm not usually, I swear. My character tends toward blitheness and optimism, or at least it used to. I look at my trajectory—a turbulent childhood, a house without much money, no family history of postsecondary education—and I'm proud of what I have accomplished. I look at the feminism I embraced as a young woman in the early nineties, the so-called "empowerment" years, with its gospel of personal emancipation: If I just used this soap, worked out at this club, wore these heels, read this self-help manual, I would be a free woman. I could pole-dance my way to liberation. And I could do it on my own and have a nest egg to show for it.

How empty that promise seems now. I had my eye on individual freedom, while ignoring the ways in which the systems exploited the vast majority of people who toiled in it—women, yes, but men, too. They are also crushed by a machine that values only the profit that can be extracted from them.

Perhaps this realization is dawning. Perhaps I can claw out a little hope from that most-maligned demographic group, millennials (that is, people born in the twenty-year period beginning in the early 1980s). Through their lack of material acquisitiveness, millennials have been accused of ruining, among other things, car ownership, home ownership, golf, cruise ships, and napkins. Elsewhere in the book, I've noted that some of them have retrograde notions about gender roles in relationships. Not all, of course.

If anything, the millennials' fabled devotion to self-actualization might save us. They believe in social justice. They are not so sure about working themselves into the cardiac ward of the nearest hospital. Battered by unforgiving economic forces, they're not convinced about this whole capitalism thing. According to a 2016 study from Harvard University, 51 percent of respondents, who were between the ages of eighteen and twenty-nine, did not support capitalism; 42 percent said they did. As the *Washington Post* noted, somewhat dryly, in its accompanying story: "Capitalism can mean different things to different people, and the newest generation of voters is frustrated with the status quo, broadly speaking."

Frustrated: that's putting it mildly. Ask the young feminists who are running for office in record numbers, pushed to action by Donald Trump's misogyny. Ask the young women who are making alliances across race and class lines, realizing that traditionally marginalized allies need to be brought to the podium when strategies are planned.

I'm given hope when I listen to those young feminists, some of whom I've written about in this book or elsewhere: the ones fighting against harassment, or child marriage, or sexual violence as a tool of war. They are waging daily battles for reproductive rights or for better toilet facilities in the developing world so that girls will continue to go to school after they get their periods. They are heroes, all, and they face the future.

But I find inspiration in the past as well, as I've also tried to demonstrate in this book. Women's struggles and solidarity have been overlooked until recently, their triumphs relegated to the domestic zone.

Women's groups are thinking about ways in which social justice can be implemented on a larger, collective scale, as a way of addressing inequalities that goes beyond the narrow confines of individual empowerment. There are feminist economists working on new and enlightened ways of calculating value and productivity; feminist peace activists campaigning against arms proliferation; feminist politicians looking at innovative ways of collaborating on public policy.

As much as I look to the future, I also look for transformative wisdom from the past. I think about one of my great heroes, and a hero to great many Canadians, Ursula Franklin. Franklin, who died in 2017 at the age of ninety-four, was a renaissance woman whose paci-fism, feminism, and devotion to science combined in one singular, mighty heart. A Holocaust survivor who emigrated from Germany to Canada in 1949, she became a Quaker and spent her life opposing war in all its forms. Trained as a physicist, she became the first female professor of metallurgy and material sciences at the University of Toronto, where she unflaggingly supported other women in a profession that was not entirely hospitable to them.

In her collected essays, *The Ursula Franklin Reader: Pacifism as a Map*, she is a much more elegant cartog-rapher of the place where technology, power, and justice meet than I ever could be. In particular, she lays out a vision for a future that I find incredibly compelling. A meaningful life, she told a Women and Peace confer-ence in 1994, is one that is free of the fear of exploitation: "Peace is not the absence of war. Peace is the absence of fear. Peace is the presence of justice."

She continues: "The issues before us are very much issues of peace and justice: justice for people and justice with respect to the environment. Such justice allows a condition where there is freedom from fear: fear of war and the military; fear of economic, political, cultural or sexual oppression; fear of not knowing where to find meaningful work for oneself or one's children; fear of not knowing where there could be a public sphere in which the issues of peace and justice have priority over the issues of profit."

How to engineer such a world? That's the question. Maybe some of the answers are being incubated right now in the Toronto high school named after Ursula Franklin; students lucky enough to win a spot there are taught a curriculum heavy on science, social justice, and free thought.

Maybe the answer is in the head of the physics graduate student who asked Franklin if there was a place in science for a young feminist. Yes, Franklin wrote back, the exact right place for a young feminist was in science. She wrote to the graduate student, addressed only as Marcia, in a letter published in 1993: "Take the time to keep involved in women's issues, and don't ever think of yourself as 'the only woman in...' Likely you are not, just as I have never been. Wherever men work, there are also women working, usually for much lower pay. You may be the only female doctoral student in a particular group, but what about the secretaries, the cleaning staff, the librarians and the technicians? You may link up with them and gain their support and friendship. As you watch over the safety and well-being of others, your own will take care of itself and the chilly climate will warm up a bit."

I will confess that it makes me teary to read that passage, almost twenty-five years after it was first published. How chilly it still is for women out there, especially women in technology, science, and computer engineering. As I write this, the news is filled with stories of the harassment and abuse that women in tech continue to suffer. Their very right to be in those industries is still questioned. And yet, as Marge Piercy noted, those who control the technology control the direction of a society. It is crucial for women to be present at the inception of the imagined future.

Even if the promise of Ursula Franklin's letter to her student is yet unfulfilled, its central message is more crucial now than ever: We must work together to change a punishing system. We must elevate the work of women who have been hidden. We must make alliances, and friendships, and open our ears to new voices. Otherwise the climate will remain chilly; and you know who will be frozen out.

SIZE MATTERS:
A COMMENCEMENT ADDRESS

IN MY DREAMS, I am called upon. Not to lead an army or make enough cupcakes for the entire class picnic—no, nothing so worthy. In my dreams, I am called to give a commencement speech.

I know: sad! Feel free to say it together: *how very sad*. Who else would dream of standing on a podium in front of hundreds of recent graduates desperate to tear off their smelly rented gowns and ravage the first beer keg they see? Who else dreams of being asked by their university to return and scatter platitudes like cherry blossoms on the wind?

I do, damn it. I do. Every spring, I watch in envy as the famous of the world, who do not need more free publicity, gather on leafy campuses around North America to spread their hard-won, common-sense insights. They are Johnny Appleseeds of folksy wisdom, tossing hard-earned wisdom from manicured fingers. Love! Fail! Grow! Grow to love failure!

Every spring my skepticism cowers in the back seat—normally it likes to drive—as I read famous people's commencement speeches and admit to myself that they are right. Those bromides are bright with truth. Often I'm sobbing as I realize this. You're right, George Saunders, when you say that a person's goal in life should be, simply, to be kinder. And J. K. Rowling, I agree that there is no greater teacher than failure and no greater gift than imagination. Steve Jobs, you speak the truth when you say that you must follow your heart and your instincts—wait a second, Jobs. You're a dropout! How the hell did you get to deliver a commencement address? Oh, right. You changed the landscape of the modern world.

Of all the commencement speeches that have been published in large print and stuffed into Christmas stockings around the world, none, to my mind, is greater than the one Nora Ephron delivered at her alma mater, Wellesley College, in 1996.

Ephron graduated in 1962, and she demonstrates how the world had changed by stating a few simple facts: there were five African-American women in her graduating class; the dorm-room door had to be left open six inches if a boy was in the room; six girls had been kicked out of college that year for "lesbianism." Illegal abortions cost $500 and were performed without anaesthetic. In her speech, she threw some epic shade on the Disney-bright nostalgia that enveloped postwar America.

So much had happened in Ephron's life since she graduated — the heartbreak that led to *Heartburn*, the brilliant essays, the screenplays for *Silkwood* and *When Harry Met Sally* and a dozen other films. It was a tornado of a life, and she embraced it. Her speech celebrated feminism, and accomplishment, and — my favourite part — the chaos and too-muchness of life. Here is what she says:

> Maybe young women don't wonder whether they can have it all any longer, but in case any of you are wondering, of course you can have it all. What are you going to do? Everything, is my guess. It will be a little messy, but embrace the mess. It will be complicated, but rejoice in the complications. It will not be anything like what you think it will be like, but surprises are good for you.

Sometimes, when I'm walking or having a shower or talking to my imaginary boyfriend Keith Richards, who likes to bring biscotti when he visits, I imagine what my commencement speech would say. Would I talk about how it is vital to always carry a notebook and pen? I could mention Roald Dahl's warning that "a thought unrecorded is a thought lost." I could tell the anecdote about my trainwreck interview with a Very Important Man: As I sat down to record his thoughts, I realized that the only writing utensil in my purse was my toddler son's Spider-Man pen, which squawked "With great power comes great responsibility!" every time it touched paper.

Or perhaps I should talk about how the most import-ant thing to look for in a mate is a similar tolerance for filth — or for freaks, a love of cleanliness. This, I feel, is the secret to marital bliss, and astonishingly unreported. A man who will run away screaming when he finds a desiccated mouse carcass stuck to the shag carpet under a pile of your dirty clothes is not a man who will stick around through life's other crises. I discovered this the hard way. Conversely, a man who will whisk a coffee mug filled with moldy sunflower seed shells from your bedside table with no words fur-ther than "Good morning, baby" is a man you want holding your hand at the very end. When I found this man — there was only one left in the shop — I married him.

But filth and emergency preparedness are such little topics. The graduates of tomorrow — particularly the women, at whom this book is aimed — should be thinking about living large. Yes, that's what I'd talk about, if only some enterprising college administrator would ask me to expound on the topic. What, you'd like to hear it anyway? Bless you. Bless you, my imaginary friend.

This is what I'd say:

Good afternoon, and welcome everyone on this beautiful afternoon. It's so wonderful to be back on this campus after so many years. I was starting to think I'd been banned, it's been so long! Not that I'm bitter at all, and I regret that email I sent the dean last year, truly. I'd been feverish for three days and was living on cough medicine and vodka.

It is a great honour and privilege to be with you here today. You've made it, and well done to all of you. You don't have to listen to some ancient alumna drone on at you about boring historical events any longer — except for the next few minutes. Seriously, don't try to leave. I've been waiting for this moment for decades. There are guards at all the exits.

How little this campus has changed — that's the

tree we used to climb at the end of one-dollar draught night. And yet how much it's changed. Do you see that building there? It used to be a women's residence. The student newspaper carried a story about how the fire exits were kept locked because the administrators were more worried about boys getting in than women trapped by fire getting out. It's true! What a crazy old world.

And that building over there — we used to be able to smoke inside. I smoked with a professor who had worked on Fleet Street and who told me I should never wear stripes because they made me look fat. He used to make the female students do spins for him, like we were fashion models. It's true! What a strange old world it was.

I took that professor's words to heart, for some strange reason. I went on a crash diet in my last year of school and lost 20 pounds by eating only Hickory Sticks and drinking only beer. It was not a hospital-certified diet. Of course, I was also diagnosed with a life-threatening, incurable disease at the same time, but who cared! I was thin, for once. I was the subject of admiring glances. I had shrunk myself, and therefore grown in attractiveness, and desirability. What strange mathematics this was, that I had never been taught!

Years later, while working as a newspaper reporter,

I would sit across from a man who regularly shushed me. I know what you're thinking: How am I standing here, delivering this commencement address, and not in prison for this man's murder? It's crazy! There were many days when I would open my mouth and he would frown at me across the desk divider and hold his finger to his lips, and I would think, *I wonder if this stapler could kill a person?* Or, *Could this Diet Coke can be used to crack open a skull?* And yet I never did. I was afraid of jail, my friends. And I was so young. I actually thought, in those days, that if I made myself smaller and quieter—if I reduced my footprint in the world—then I would be happier.

No, I lie. I didn't think I would make myself happier. I thought I'd make the people around me happier. If only I were less lippy. If only my laugh were quieter. If only my boobs were smaller, perhaps men would stop talking to them. It would shrink the target, at least. If I had no opinions, no one could criticize me. Shrinking and hiding is an excellent defence strategy, as every prey animal knows.

As Chimamanda Ngozi Adichie once said, "We teach girls to shrink themselves, to make themselves smaller."

I did try, for a little while, to be smaller and quieter. It never lasted, though. I was too lazy. No one tells you the effort that is required in diminishment; it takes an enormous amount of energy to constrict yourself. Sometimes I like to think of those women in history and what they could have accomplished if their lungs weren't compressed by corsets, their feet mangled to fit into tiny doll's shoes. How they could have shouted. How they could have run.

So what I would like to say to you young women out there is: Be large. Be as large as you'd like to be. Take up the room that is yours. Spread into every crack and corner and wide plain of this magnificent world. Sit with your legs apart on the subway until a man is forced, politely, to ask you to slide over so he can have a seat. Get the dressing on the salad. Get two dressings. Order the ribs on a first date.

Throw away your scale. Stop weighing yourself. Is there ever a reason to know your precise weight? Are you mailing yourself to China? Are you a bag of cocaine? Enjoy your mass, for one day you will be old and as shrivelled as an apple doll, and you will wonder where the rest of you went. Wear a tiny bathing suit, even if the sales clerk raises her eyebrow when you try it on. Especially if she raises her eyebrow. Wear a small dress on your large self.

Be loud, in your head and in public. In meetings, speak first and resist the temptation to preface every statement with "This may have already been brought up..." When a colleague tries to interrupt, hold up a hand and say, "I'll be finished making my point shortly, Bob," and try not to picture what he'd look like with a stapler embedded in his forehead.

Laugh as loudly as you'd like during movies and live performances. Do not put your hand over your mouth. You aren't vomiting or letting the devil in. You're laughing. It is a sign of approval, like undoing your pants after a particularly fine meal.

Take up all the space. It is your space. There will be people who try to drive you from it, with catcalls or derision, with mockery and disapproval. These things diminish them, not you. Do not allow yourself to be diminished. Expand like a flower, like a heated gas, like a beautiful rising loaf. Expand into yourself, and never apologize for it.

And for the young men in the crowd, who already know by some strange alchemy how to be large and expansive, I would say this: Let your sisters in this world grow, too, and do not consider their growth to be a diminishment of yours. The world is not a zero-sum game, and there is cake enough for everyone. Be the bigger man, and welcome the bigger woman.

That's all I have to say today. I want to wish you all a large and happy future.

NOTES

INTRODUCTION: TALES FOR YOUNG WITCHES

Gay, Roxane. *Bad Feminist: Essays*. London: Corsair, 2014.

de Beauvoir, Simone. *The Second Sex*. London: Vintage Classics, 2015.

Zeisler, Andi. *We Were Feminists Once: From Riot Grrrl to Covergirl®, The Buying & Selling of a Political Movement*. New York: Public Affairs, 2016.

Grant, Tavia. "Who Is Minding the Gap?" *Globe and Mail*, March 6, 2017.

Reich, Robert, and Heather McCulloch. "Wealth, Not Just Wages, Is the Way to Measure Women's Equality." *Los Angeles Times*, August 25, 2017.

Boesveld, Sarah. "68% of Canadian Women Don't Call Themselves a Feminist." *Chatelaine*, December 17, 2015. www.chatelaine.com.

Cai, Weiyi, and Scott Clement. "What Americans Think About Feminism Today." *Washington Post*, January 27, 2016.

THE WAY OF THE HARASSER

Eltahawy, Mona. *Headscarves and Hymens: Why the Middle East Needs a Sexual Revolution.* Toronto: HarperCollins, 2015.

UN Women. "Safe Cities Global Initiative Report." Report, 2015. doi: www.unwomen.org/en/digital-library /publications/2015/9/proceedings-report-un-womens-safe-cities-global-leaders-forum-2015.

Stop Street Harassment. "Unsafe and Harassed in Public Spaces: A National Street Harassment Report." Report, 2014. doi: http://www.stopstreetharassment.org/wp-content /uploads/2012/08/2014-National-SSH-Street-Harassment -Report.pdf.

Livingston, Beth, Maria Grillo, and Rebecca Paluch, "Cornell University International Study on Street Harassment." Report, May 2015. doi: https://www.ihollaback.org/cornell -international-survey-on-street-harassment.

Foster, Dawn. "If I Ever See You in the Street, I Hope You Get Shot." *London Review of Books*, May 27, 2016.

West, Lindy. *Shrill: Notes From a Loud Woman.* New York: Hachette, 2016.

Moran, Caitlin. *Moranifesto*. London: Ebury Press, 2016.

Phillips, Jess. *Everywoman: One Woman's Truth About Speaking Out*. London: Hutchinson, 2017.

Amnesty International UK. "Black and Asian Women MPs Abused More Online." Report, September 2017. doi: https://www.amnesty.org.uk/online-violence-women-mps.

Quinn, Zoe. *Crash Override: How Gamergate (Nearly) Destroyed My Life and How We Can Win the Fight Against Online Hate*. New York: PublicAffairs, 2017.

FEARLESSNESS

Bellafante, Ginia. "The False Feminism of 'Fearless Girl.'" *New York Times*, March 16, 2017.

Bourke, Joanna. *Fear: A Cultural History*. London: Virago, 2005.

AMBITION: THREE LIFE LESSONS

Franklin, Miles. *My Brilliant Career*. London: William Blackwood and Sons, 1901. (Adapted for film by Gillian Armstrong; released 1979.)

Coontz, Stephanie. "Do Millennial Men Want Stay-at-Home Wives?" *New York Times*, March 31, 2017.

Bursztyn, Leonardo, Thomas Fujiwara, and Amanda Pallais, "'Acting Wife': Marriage Market Incentives and Labor Market Investments.'" *American Economic Review*, 2017.

Smith, Vivian. *Outsiders Still: Why Women Journalists Love and Leave Their Newspaper Careers*. Toronto: University of Toronto Press, 2015.

Abouzahr, Katie, Matt Krentz, Frances Brooks Taplett, Claire Tracey, and Miki Tsusaka. "Dispelling the Myths of the Gender 'Ambition Gap,'" April 5, 2017. Boston Consulting Group. https://www.bcg.com/en-ca/publications/2017/people-organization-leadership-change-dispelling-the-myths-of-the-gender-ambition-gap.aspx.

Slaughter, Anne-Marie. *Unfinished Business: Women Men Work Family*. New York: Random House, 2015.

YOU'LL PAY FOR THOSE BREASTS, OR THE COST OF BEING A LADY

Wolf, Naomi. *The Beauty Myth: How Images of Beauty Are Used Against Women*. London: Vintage Classics, 2015.

Mistry, Meenal. "The High Price of Beauty: 4 Women Reveal Their Annual Costs." *Wall Street Journal*, January 8, 2016.

Morrissey, Tracie Egan. "This Is How Much It Costs to Own a Vagina: An Itemized List," *Jezebel,* April 6, 2012. https://jezebel.com/5890058/this-is-how-much-it-costs-to-own-a-vagina-an-itemized-list.

New York City Department of Consumer Affairs. "From Cradle to Cane: The Cost of Being a Female Consumer." Study, December 2015. http://www1.nyc.gov/site/dca/partners/gender-pricing-study.page.

NEVER ENOUGH: WOMEN, POLITICS, AND
THE UPHILL BATTLE

Coletto, David. "Finding Parity: Canadian Opinions About Women in Politics." Abacus Data, March 6, 2017. http://abacusdata.ca/finding-parity-canadian-opinions-about-women-in-politics.

Carstairs, Sharon, and Tim Higgins. *Dancing Backwards: A Social History of Canadian Women in Politics*. Winnipeg: Heartland Associates, 2004.

UN News Centre. "UN Reports Slow Women's Political Parity," UN News Centre, March 15, 2017. http://www.un.org/apps/news/story.asp?NewsID=56357#.Wg8dwLQ-cQ8.

Inter-Parliamentary Union. "Women in Politics: 2017." Report, March 2017. https://www.ipu.org/resources/publications/infographics/2017-03/women-in-politics-2017.

Oxfam Canada. "Feminist Scorecard 2017." Report, March 2017. https://www.oxfam.ca/our-work/publications/time-to-turn-feminist-words-into-action.

Rosenbluth, Frances, Joshua Kalla, and Dawn Teele. "The Female Political Career," Women in Parliaments and The World Bank, January 2015. http://www.worldbank.org/en/news/feature/2015/01/27/the-female-political-career-women-members-of-parliament-still-face-obstacles-to-elected-office.

Gillard, Julia. "Julia Gillard Speaks in London in Memory of Jo Cox MP." Blog, October 11, 2016. http://juliagillard.com.au/articles/julia-gillard-speaks-in-memory-of-jo-cox-mp/.

Beard, Mary. "Women in Power," *London Review of Books*, March 16, 2017.

IF THE WORLD WERE MADE OF LEGO: A LETTER TO MY SON

hooks, bell. *Feminism Is for Everybody: Passionate Politics*. New York: Routledge, 2015.

UNBALANCED

Duxbury, Linda, and Chris Higgins. "Work–Life Conflict in Canada in the New Millennium: A Status Report," October 2003, http://publications.gc.ca/collections/Collection/H72 -21-186-2003E.pdf.

Schulte, Brigid. *Overwhelmed: Work, Love, and Play When No One Has the Time*. Toronto: HarperCollins, 2014.

Cansever, Edip. "Table." Translated by Robert Tillinghast. *The Stonecutter's Hand*. Boston: David R. Godine, Inc., 1995.

Phillips, Adam. *On Balance*. New York: Farrar, Straus and Giroux, 2010.

THE STORY OF MY MOTHER

Gordon, Charlotte. *Romantic Outlaws: The Extraordinary Lives of Mary Wollstonecraft & Mary Shelley*. New York: Random House, 2015.

Wilder, Laura Ingalls. *Little House on the Prairie*. New York: Harper Trophy, 2004.

Fisher, Carrie. *Wishful Drinking*. London: Pocket Books, 2009.

FOUR LIONS

Greer, Germaine. *Shakespeare's Wife*. Toronto: McClelland & Stewart, 2008.

———. *The Female Eunuch*. London: Harper Perennial, 2006.

James, P. D. *The Lighthouse*. Toronto: Knopf Canada, 2005.

———. *Time to Be in Earnest*. Toronto: Knopf Canada, 2001.

———. *The Private Patient*. Toronto: Knopf Canada, 2008.

———. *Death Comes to Pemberley*. Toronto: Knopf Canada, 2011.

Mantel, Hilary. *Wolf Hall*. London: Fourth Estate, 2009.

———. *Bring Up the Bodies*. London: Fourth Estate, 2012.

———. *Giving Up the Ghost: A Memoir*. London: Harper Perennial, 2004.

A VIEW FROM THE OUTSIDE: A LETTER TO MY YOUNGER SELF

Gay, Roxane. *Hunger*. New York: HarperCollins, 2017.

McKeon, Lauren. *F-Bomb: Dispatches from the War on Feminism*. Fredericton: Goose Lane Editions, 2017.

THE LONG CRAWL TO DEFEAT, THE SLOW MARCH TO VICTORY

Wayne, Carly, Marzia Oceno, and Nicholas Valentino. "How Sexism Drives Support for Donald Trump," *Washington Post*, October 23, 2016.

Clinton, Hillary. *What Happened*. New York: Simon & Schuster, 2017.

KILLER ROBOTS, AMAZON PLANETS, AND THE FIGHT FOR THE FUTURE

Atkinson, Kate. *A God in Ruins*. Toronto: Doubleday Canada, 2015.

Sandel, Michael. *What Money Can't Buy: The Moral Limits of Markets*. London: Allen Lane, 2012.

Atwood, Margaret. *The Handmaid's Tale*. Toronto: McClelland & Stewart, 2014.

Edelman. "2017 Edelman Trust Barometer." Global Annual Study, January 15, 2017. www.edelman.com.

Piercy, Marge. *Woman on the Edge of Time*. New York: Ballantine, 2016.

Harari, Yuval Noah. *Homo Deus: A Brief History of Tomorrow*. London: Vintage 2017.

Ehrenfreund, Max. "A Majority of Millennials Now Reject Capitalism, Poll Shows," *Washington Post*, April 26, 2016.

Franklin, Ursula M. *The Ursula Franklin Reader: Pacifism as a Map*. Toronto: Between the Lines, 2006.

SIZE MATTERS: A COMMENCEMENT ADDRESS

George Saunders delivered the commencement address at Syracuse University in 2013; J. K. Rowling at Harvard University in 2008; Steve Jobs at Stanford University in 2005; Nora Ephron at Wellesley College in 1996; and my speech was delivered at no university, ever, which is why it's included here.

ACKNOWLEDGEMENTS

ON THE NIGHT after the U.S. presidential election in November 2016, I went to dinner at my publisher Sarah MacLachlan's house. If you imagine that the mood was dire, you would be erring on the side of optimism. Sarah, wise and resilient, was determined that we should not roll over and be crushed by the moment. I'd written a column for the *Globe and Mail* that day, wondering what we could possibly tell our daughters that would explain the rise of a toxic misogynist to the most powerful position in the world.

"You should write that book," Sarah said. A book about women's lives, and contemporary feminism, told through the lens of my own life and experience. Maybe with some laughs thrown in so that we didn't drown in tears. I sat down with my marvellous editor Janie Yoon to shape the course of this book. Sarah and Janie are my navigators; I bow down before them.

Every journalist's life is made up of stories. No stories, no life—no professional life, anyway. In this book I've combined my own stories with those that have been shared with me, so generously, by people over the years. My calcified heart melts a bit when I think of all those who have shared their experiences, thoughts, and dreams with me, without asking anything in return. I extend my deepest and most profound gratitude to anyone who's ever given me an interview, and especially to the women whose words are included in this book.

To all the friends whose stories I have also included in this book—sorry. But also, thanks! Those were good times.

I've been blessed, over the years, to have the dull metal of my prose improved through some alchemy by a host of wonderful newspaper and magazine editors, many of them women. At the start of my career were two mentors, Katherine Ashenburg and Cathrin Bradbury, whom I am lucky to count as friends today. I cannot tell you how much their wisdom and support has meant to me. As well, I think of the female editors I've been lucky enough to work with over the years (though they may have a different view of things as they toil in the dark salt mines of my writing). A brief list would include: Natasha Hassan, Noreen Rasbach, Carol Toller, Sue Grimbly, Kim Izzo, Suzanne Boyd, Christina Vardanis, Stevie Cameron, Leanne Delap, Lisan Jutras, Denise Balkissoon, Shawna Richer, Sheree-Lee Olson, Amberly McAteer, Sherrill Sutherland, and many others too numerous to name. I apologize to those I've somehow overlooked. There have been many wonderful and supportive male editors over the years, too, but I'm running out of room.

Dear friends who have provided invaluable comfort, in addition to the above, include Sarah, Kim, Stephanie, Karen, Johanna, Ellen, Martha, Jane, my friend and mentee Hannah, the witchy genius writers of the Coven, the women who play Man in the Hat, the boss ladies from London, and my darling Karen from Los Angeles. I owe you all a cocktail or three.

My colleagues and friends at the *Globe and Mail* have been an inspiration over the many years I've worked with them. I am equally lucky when it comes to my book publisher, and I extend my gratitude to every hard-working, cheery, inventive person at House of Anansi who helped bring this book baby into the world, including copy editor Tracy Bordian, managing editor Maria Golikova, designer Alysia Shewchuk, and publicist Holley Corfield. I'm grateful also for the encouragement and support of my agent, John Pearce.

Whatever sanity I retain is thanks to my extraordinary family. I could not have chosen a better group than the one genetics randomly selected for me. Thanks above all to my splendid mother, Mildred, whose zest, vivacity, and sheer appetite for knowledge have been a constant inspiration. Without her these essays wouldn't exist. My mother-in-law, Pat, and father-in-law, Lu, are a source of joy and support always. My sisters and brothers, as well as my nieces and nephews, provide a network of warmth and happiness.

While I was writing this book, I lost one of the most important people in my life: My older brother Steven became ill as I began the project and died not long after. He was, in the words of his friend, "such a good man." His presence — as a scholar, friend, person of integrity, teller of off-colour jokes — will remain with me always.

Finally, right at the centre of my life are the three people who give it meaning: my husband, Doug, who is reader, partner, dispenser of Scotch, and awesome man in one package; and our children, Griff and Maud, the winning tickets in the lottery of my life.

ELIZABETH RENZETTI is a columnist for the *Globe and Mail*. She has also been the newspaper's Arts and Books editor, and reported for several years from London and Los Angeles. She is the author of the novel *Based on a True Story*, which was a finalist for the Kobo Emerging Writer Prize and a Canadian bestseller. She lives in Toronto with her husband, author and *Globe and Mail* columnist Doug Saunders, their two children, and a cat named Perdu who keeps getting lost.